Cate Murray
caryandcate.com

Outskirts of the Woods

Poems, Plays, Essays & a Biography

by Dr. Catherine T. Murray   ©2020

Dedicated to Cary Nichols

Contents

Bertha's Butter Club

A One-Act Comedy by Cate Murray

Characters:

Bertha – has suffered 20 years of weight gain and loss as well as a four year addiction to bulimia. As the play opens, Bertha feels triumphant as she has recently lost 80 pounds, and she has her bulimia under control. She works on a master's degree in counseling and plans to focus on weight issues. She views herself as a leader (although she is generally humorless) and calls together a group of overweight friends. Bertha believes she can solve their problems.

Naomi – she is a nurse engaged to a bariatric physician named Kyle. Kyle sends Naomi constant messages about her need to lose weight. Naomi has second thoughts about the man she loves.

Sita – the most overweight of the group who eats without awareness. Her family settled in the U. S. from Northern India. Because of Sita's excess weight, the family has been unable to arrange a marriage for her.

Judy – a happily married 70 year old who has always been overweight.

Helice – deals with her weight issues by humor much to Bertha's chagrin. Helice and Bertha have known each other from elementary school, and they annoy each other.

<u>Scene 1</u> Naomi's den
Naomi and Sita sit at a table. Naomi breaks open fortune cookies
and reads the weight-related "fortune" in each one. Sita quickly
eats the broken cookies.

Naomi

[Breaks open a cookie and reads] Three thousand, five hundred calories that are not expended by exercise or mental pursuits equal one pound of fat. [With some disgust] I learned that in my pre-nursing nutrition course!

Sita

[With part of a cookie in her mouth] How often does Kyle send these messages?

Naomi

Every other day! I wish he would focus on his patients.

Sita

Do you mean patients like the people he takes care of, or patience like being more patient with you?

Naomi

Both! Now listen to this one: "Obesity triples the chances of heart disease, breast cancer, hemorrhoids, and sexual dysfunction." The only one sexually dysfunctional in this relationship is Kyle. He's not manly enough to get aroused by a fat fiancèe!

Sita

Are you sure you want to marry him?

Naomi

I'm having my doubts. I'm tempted to just not show up for the ceremony. [Breaks open another cookie and Sita picks up the pieces and eats them.]

Sita

I've heard of grooms not showing for the wedding, but not brides...except for that movie with Julia Roberts – years ago – what was it called? The Runaway Bride! And wasn't there a real runaway bride on the news?

Naomi

I'm not going to run away. I'll stay right here and arrange for a date with a real man who appreciates real women! Ohhhh...of all the men in the universe to fall in love with, why do I need to pick a bariatric physician? (Looks at Sita and pauses) Are you sure you want to eat those cookies? They're sugar-free **and** low-fat. Yuck!

[Doorbell rings and Naomi slowly gets up and answers it. Helice comes in wearing a conspiratorial smile. She wears a tee that reads, "I'm really bulimic. I just haven't learned to throw up yet!"]

Helice

Hey ladies! [Drops her smile] You look really sad, Naomi. Did Dr. Killjoy e-mail you again?

Naomi

This time he sent the messages in fortune cookies. Look. [Shows a message to Helice. Helice reads it and tosses it on the floor.]

Sita

At least the fortune cookies are good. They taste good to me even though they're fat-free and sugar-free.

[Helice picks up the container and reads the container.]

Helice
It's just like Kyle to send laxatives in a gift package.

Sita
Laxatives!

Helice
Yeah, that's what chemically altered sugar is, especially if you eat more than two cookies.

Naomi
Sita has eaten almost the whole package. Not that I mind. I won't touch them.

Helice
Well Sita, tomorrow you might spend some time in the bathroom getting rid of excess weight. And Naomi, you need to get rid of Kyle the same way!

Naomi
Wish I could!

Helice
I know why Kyle is the way he is! It's not just his medical training. I blame Hollywood and the fashion industry. Really though, fat hasn't always been ugly. Look at all the Old Masters' paintings!

Naomi

Reubens especially like the queen-sized ladies! I think I'll order a Reubens' print bathroom curtain. I'd love to see Kyle's face when he sees it!

Helice

Decorate your new home Reubensesque! The other night I met this really cool dude...or I thought he was cool. We had a great time talking. I invited him over to my place. He wasn't familiar with my neighborhood, so I drew him a map. Do you want to know what the jerk said to me? He looked at the map and laughed. Laughed! He said, "This is a fat girl's map. Look at the landmarks: here's Taco Bell, Dolores' Donut Shop, Paolo's Pizza!" I tore up the map and left the bar!

Sita

I've had very few dates in my life. In my culture marriages are arranged. My parents tried to negotiate a marriage for me on four different occasions. Each prospective groom greeted me at the door and looked me over vertically and horizontally. Each one politely stayed until the end of the evening, but I knew right away that there would be no wedding. [Pauses] I've never been kissed.

Helice

I didn't get kissed till I was 18. I think guys are afraid that if they kiss a fat girl, they'll get fat. But let's change the subject. Help me finish this great poem I started.

[Doorbell rings again. Naomi opens the door for Judy. Judy holds an empty casserole dish.]

Judy

[Hands the dish to Naomi] Thanks a million, Naomi! Eddie and I both loved the herbal chicken. You must share the recipe. I didn't dare tell Eddie that it was low fat!

Naomi

Of course! The recipe comes from one of the thousands of weight loss blogs I read. Judy, I want you to meet Sita and Helice. Judy is my best neighbor.

[Naomi takes the casserole dish into the next room.]

Judy

It's great to finally meet you two. I love your tee shirt, Helen. [Laughs as she reads] Tacky but so funny.

Helice

My name's actually Helice, H-E-L-I-C-E. Helice is a little-known classical name, an ancient Greek nymph who was changed into the Big Dipper. I guess that's why I am so big! I can blame my extra pounds on my name and on my parents who named me! [All laugh.] If you like my tee, Judy, you'll love the new poem I started. [Pulls the poem out and reads.] "I founded a new political cause: It's called SEX FOR THE OVERWEIGHT! You don't have to be directly involved to join." It goes a little downhill from there. Help me fix it. How about a line about sumo wrestlers? You know, those enormous Japanese guys. I hear that they can consume more than 5,000 calories a day.

Judy

I like the line about sumo wrestlers, or the idea about the line about the sumo wrestlers. [Laughs again] Reminds me of Eddie and me 50 years ago! We had only been married a month when we broke a bed! [Everyone laughs] A beautiful, antique bed. But only the slats. This Lincoln bed has been in Eddie's family for generations. It happened at my mother-in-law's house, and she gave me dirty looks for three years after that. Late that night Mother Hampton heard a thump when the mattress and box springs hit the floor. She bursts in and turns on the 100 watt light. Eddie and I were struggling to get up just as nude as Adam and Eve! I don't know if Mother Hampton blamed our weight or our libido or both!

[Everyone laughs heartily.]

Helice

Mind if I include that incident in the poem?

Judy

Be my guest! But let's not send it to my mother-in-law!

[Doorbell rings again]

Naomi

Goodness! Am I having a party that I forgot about? [Goes to answer the door. Bertha steps in.] Bertha, you look fantastic! You lost much more than 60 pounds. How much weight have you lost, if you don't mind telling?

Bertha

[Tells everyone] A year ago, I had a modest goal of losing 60 pounds. But I decided to go further. I lost 20 more pounds – eighty pounds altogether and I am now at my ideal weight. I'm working on maintaining it. [She sees Helice's tee and looks uneasily at it.]

Helice

No shit you look great! Not Big Bertha anymore! Let's go out to dinner together? My treat!

Bertha

Thanks Helice, but I'm waiting a few weeks before I go out to eat anywhere. Too many temptations. And the portions at restaurants are always too big.

Helice

That's funny. I have to go to an all-you-can-eat buffet in order to get filled. When I was a kid, my folks would send me to Weight Watchers Camp in the summer. While there, I would have fantasies about going to weight gaining camp!

Sita

You went to Weight Watchers Camp too? I had the same type of dreams at camp – pile and piles of ice cream…

Bertha

[Interrupting Sita] Ladies! I'm here to propose a weight-loss support club. If I can do it, you can do it! We can beat The Biggest Loser, Jenny Craig. We can beat them all.

Naomi

Not to interrupt, Bertha, but I want you to meet Judy. Judy, this is Bertha. Judy is my neighbor and a wonderful friend.

Judy

I'm delighted to meet you, Bertha. I'm very interested in a weight loss group.

Bertha

It's amazing what a troupe of friends can do for each other – energy, synergy, support and success! All together, Ladies [Naomi, Sita and Judy and chime in] Energy, Synergy, Support and Success!

Helice

Ever consider taking up cheerleading, Bertha?

Sita

I don't know about another group. I've tried and tried to lose weight.

Bertha

So have I, Sita! Believe me, I tried every diet in the book. Whenever I would lose control of my diet, I would feel disgusted with myself.

Sita

I gain weight thinking about food.

Bertha

I used to think I had a terrible metabolism too. Some people actually do, but Marisa, my therapist, helped me understand that the problem was my emotional attachment to food. Instead of working on my issues, I began throwing up. I felt disgusted with myself, and the disgust led to bulimia. I could have accidentally killed myself by choking on my own vomit. Marisa sensed I was in danger and she helped me get out. I could not have lost 80 pounds without her. But now I need you ladies for support.

Helice

You sure do need support! You're so thin, you're about to blow away.

Judy

I would love to join a group. When do we start?

Bertha

Would tomorrow evening be too soon?

Sita

That would be fine with me.

Naomi

Tomorrow night would be terrific! A good excuse for breaking my date with Kyle.

Helice

I guess I'll show up too. There's safety in numbers.

Bertha

Great! Let's all meet at 7:00 sharp at my place. If you have exercise mats, bring them.

Judy

I have an old yoga mat, but I'm not very limber any more.

Bertha

I'm not as agile as I was on the middle school drill team, but so what! We'll make the moves we can and enjoy ourselves!

Sita

I'll give it a try.

Judy

I second that!

Helice

This group that we are about to form deserves a proper name. How about Bertha's Butter Club?

Naomi

Helice, knock it off!

Helice

Naomi, you sound like Wally Cleaver! No, I intend the name to be positive. Butter is rich and delicious. As we lose our fat cells, we'll appreciate our small rations of butter.

Judy

Bertha's Butter Club sounds cute, if you're not offended, Bertha.

Bertha

I'm not offended. [Although she really is.] Sounds a little silly though.

Sita

Let's be silly.

[The doorbell rings.]

Naomi

Crap, I hope it's not Kyle. [She goes to answer the door.]

Helice

If it is, I'll flirt with him and scare him away!

[Naomi answers the door. Unseen, a female pizza deliverer comically sings the order.]

Deliverer

Two extra-large specials – Canadian bacon, Italian sausage, and triple cheese!

Naomi

I didn't order anything!

Helice

I did! Let's indulge before we starve! (Helice pays the deliverer, and Naomi grabs some plates. Sita takes one.)

Bertha

No, wait a minute. The best time to start healthy eating is now...No really, you have the will power!

[Judy looks undecided at first, and then takes a plate. The other women ignore Bertha. Lights out. End of scene.]

<u>Scene 2</u> Bertha's den
In the background is a recording of Henry Mancini's "Baby Elephant Walk." Bertha, Naomi, Judy, and Sita all move to the music. Bertha and Naomi dance 60's style. Judy is sitting and moves one arm then the other holding lightweight barbells. After a while, Bertha gets up and turns off the music.

Bertha

Great, Ladies! We exercised 15 minutes tonight. Anyone out of breath? (The others raise their hands and pat their chests.) You'll soon be used to exertion. We'll exercise 30 minutes next week, for the next two weeks. After two weeks, we can exercise 45 minutes. Soon we'll be up to an hour! Now I want all of you to stand up. (Bertha waits for all to stand.) Now, very, very slowly inhale and exhale. (Bertha loudly demonstrates, and the others follow suit for a few times.) Remember Scarlett O'Hara in Gone with the Wind?

Judy

Eddie and I saw it five times! We have the DVD at home.

Bertha

Great old film, isn't it? Remember the scene, just before intermission, when Scarlett raises her right hand, like this (demonstrates) in a power fist and says, "As God is my witness, I'll never be hungry again!"

Sita

I remember that scene! Didn't Scarlett just try to eat an unwashed turnip – the only thing growing in the garden? I could eat an unwashed turnip right now. I only ate salad with tofu at 5:30.

Naomi

Don't forget the crackers you ate at my house – about 250 calories worth.

Sita

I ate that many?

Naomi

You eat without knowing it, Sita. Your mind is elsewhere while you eat.

Judy

I need a bracelet around my wrist that shocks when I reach for food.

Bertha

You don't need a bracelet, any of you. You're all strong women. You will lose weight and keep it off. Be more aware of food, Sita. Now Ladies, repeat after me: "As God is my witness, I'll never be fat again!"

Judy

As God is my witness, I'll never be fat again!

Sita

As Shiva and Shakti are my witnesses, I'll never be fat or hungry again!

Bertha

Sita is right about one thing. Although it's good to quit eating after supper, it's best not to get too hungry. We don't want low blood sugar!

Judy

I heard that some murders have been blamed on low blood sugar. Years ago, didn't some defense attorney argue a case called the "Twinkie defense"?

Bertha

I think the attorney said it was due to high blood sugar.

Naomi

I don't know how valid the Twinkie defense was, but I could kill for a cheese Danish right now.

Sita

I'll take a Dove bar!

Judy

Honestly, I'm tempted to go to Waffle House and eat everything in sight!

Bertha

Let's practice willpower instead. Think of how beautiful your bodies will be in a few months.

Judy

Sometimes the power of food suggestion just takes over. Years ago, I read this book – this true story about this doctor's wife who becomes mysteriously sick and dies. The doctor injected diseases into an eclair which he gave to his wife. But after reading the book, I was starving for an eclair. I went from grocery store to grocery store to find one. When I got home, Eddie was so mad!

Bertha

Ladies, we need to quit talking about food, especially empty calories. Right now we need to focus on exercise and change. Naomi, it's your turn to take the pledge.

Naomi

Not I! I'm not using the words fat or overweight, even in a positive context.

Bertha

Why not? I was fat for over 20 years.

Naomi

All my life, others have been obsessed with my fatness. In school I received valentines with cartoon hippopotamuses in tutus!

Judy

Hippos in tutus. They're in the classic Disney movie, Fantasia. They're cute.

Naomi

I don't care how cute it is on the Disney film. My classmates had no right to torment me with those pictures. My grandmother called me "Five-by-five." On my eighteenth birthday she told me she did not want to see me until I was a size 10. The next time I saw her was at her funeral.

Bertha

I understand those hostile feelings. When I went to friends' birthday parties, I would get served Jell-O! The mothers conspired with my own mom to humiliate me.

Naomi

Or they were trying to help you in their own sick way. I hated going shopping with my mother. She would take smaller sized clothes from the rack and make me attempt to try them on. One time, the clerk was a mother of a boy I liked. The clerk must have made a comment about me to her son because the boy tormented me at school the next day.

Bertha

So many boys called me "Ugly." I didn't think I would ever have a boyfriend. I lost my virginity to the first boy who seemed interested. He dumped me after that. But I've lost weight and I feel beautiful for the first time in my life.

Sita

I want to lose weight to get back at the four men who dumped me at my front door. I'm going to get skinny and learn how to throw cream pies. [The others give her funny looks.] Like in the old slapstick movies.

Bertha

For a long time, I wanted to take revenge on that first boy who dumped me. He was always stealing Cutty Sark from his dad, and I thought about spiking it with Ipecac. Sita, we've both been hurt. Let's work through pain constructively and stop the cycle of abuse.

Sita

You are my friend and I feel vengeful for your sake. Whoever that boy was, he's probably a fat man now. I'm tempted to send him cartoons of fat men, anonymously of course.

Bertha

Revenge is never sweet, Sita, but losing weight is. Do it and you'll get boyfriends, if that's what you want.

Sita

I may already have a boyfriend! A pen pal at least. His name is Jeremy. He wanted a picture of me, so I sent him one, and he wrote me back! He said I had beautiful eyes and hair. No one ever said that to me.

Naomi

Where does Jeremy live?

Sita

California.

Naomi

Where in California?

Sita

Mule Creek.

Judy

Mule Creek? Where the prison is?

Sita

Yes, Jeremy's in prison, but he will be out soon. He says the forgery was not his fault.

Judy

They all say they're innocent, but most are as guilty as a raccoon in a cookie jar.

Naomi

Just don't send him any money. All he needs is what he already gets – free meals and a place to sleep.

Sita

[Trying to hold back her anger] All right! All right! I'm sorry I told any of you about Jeremy. You have all had boyfriends or husbands except me. I feel like a freak sometimes! Let me just pretend that I have a boyfriend for a while. [Pauses] I realized someone in prison might be dangerous, so I got myself a private mail box.

Naomi

That was good thinking. If you want to continue writing Jeremy, I support you. You've certainly listened to all my recent ranting about Kyle. Patiently listened.

[Doorbell rings. Bertha opens the door, and Helice stumbles in. She limps.]

Helice

Ohhhhh! Do I ache! I took in my first yoga lesson. But I made it to my first weight loss club!

Bertha

But you're not supposed to be sore after hatha yoga. I yoga, you don't compete with everyone else. You only bend and stretch as far as you can go at any particular time.

Helice

Well I'm an American and I compete! But I didn't try to stand on my head. The instructor warned us that head standing is only for the very adept. Besides, I didn't want my boobs to fall over my face.

[Naomi, Judy and Sita all laugh. Helice grabs her stomach.]

If I could only get rid of the gas pain. It's been really bad lately. Yoga is supposed to rid us of gas! A month ago, I swear I could feel my gas moving around.

Naomi

Don't release your gas in here!

Bertha

Ladies, we've been off the subject of weight loss too long. Let's all sit down.

[All go to the couches and chairs. Helice sits down slowly, gets up slowly, and then puts a pillow against her back.]

All of you know the basics of losing weight. You have been told all your lives. How do you lose weight?

Helice

By pushing ourselves away from the table!

Judy

By pushing ourselves away from the table and running to a tennis court!

Helice

Hot sex!

Naomi

Expend more calories than we consume.

Bertha

Yes Naomi, and as Marisa puts it, "Running to success by knowing when to open our mouths (to food)." We must be aware of every bite that comes into our mouths.

Helice

I've been hearing about your therapist for years. When will I meet her?

Bertha

I don't know. Why don't you make an appointment with her?

Helice

[To the others] Bertha thinks everyone needs therapy. When we were in the seventh grade together, she tried to shrink the whole Girl Scout troop! Only a couple of us were so big we needed shrinking.

Bertha

[Trying to hold back anger] Some people appreciate help with their issues.

[Bertha's body language shows extreme anger. Her phone rings and she answers it.]

Bertha

Hello… [A pause] Yes. What is your name again, please? [A longer pause] Oh no! Can there be a mistake? [Pauses] I can't talk anymore. [Quickly hangs up the phone then tearfully addresses the others] **Marisa killed herself!** I can't believe it! [Breaks down. Naomi, Sita, Judy and Helice run to comfort her.]

<u>Scene 3</u>
Naomi, Judy and Sita all sit in Naomi's den.

Judy
Such a tragedy. [Touches her heart] I swallowed a stone when I heard the news. I can't imagine how Bertha feels. I haven't known her long, but I can see she depended so much on Marisa. She was so close to her!

Naomi
I'm hurting over Marisa too. I had a few sessions with her myself, last year.

Sita
That's right. I remember you making the appointments.

Naomi
Marisa helped me. I just couldn't keep going to the sessions because I didn't want to keep focusing on...I couldn't work through my pain because I wanted to forget about it. I'm just so dumbfounded as to what could have been happening in Marisa's own life.

Judy
Sometimes it's easier for people to help others than help themselves.

Naomi
I told Marisa something I've never told anyone else, not even Kyle. I need to talk about it to you, but it's really hard. [Pauses] I'm a survivor of incest – it was my dad, and I hate him for it!

Judy

Oh Naomi, I had no idea. [Holds Naomi's hand and starts crying. Sita cries also.]

[A pause]

Naomi

Thank you for crying for me. I cried by myself for years. Ever since I took Prozac, I've been unable to cry. Prozac has helped a lot of people, but all it did was seal my feelings deep inside of me.

Judy

Do you think that a group, an incest group, would help?

Naomi

Maybe our weight loss group will help me once Bertha feels like meeting again. [Pause] I don't know if anything can help. I feel so ashamed, so alienated.

Judy

It's not your fault. I love you so much, and I can almost taste blood feeling your hurt.

Sita

Parents never know how much they hurt us. I severed ties with mine. They don't have my address or my new cell number.

Naomi

I know I gained all this weight to protect myself. When I started to gain weight, Daddy Dearest would put me on the scale, naked. I smell vomit just speaking about him!

[Sita runs from the room crying. Naomi and Judy look at each other. A moment of silence. After a pause, Naomi leaves the room and returns with Sita. They all hug.]

I'm sorry, Sita. I'm sorry I hurt you.

[Pause]

Sita
I'm glad you shared your story. I need to share something I've kept in a closed book for several years. When I was 19 and still living at home, I got angry at my parents. They would not let me go out at all, except to my job. I could not convince them they were wrong. Without telling them, I spent the night with a girlfriend. When I got home, my parents were convinced I was with a boy. [Pauses] My father threatened me with a strap, and made me strip. He examined me vaginally. I was still a virgin. I'm still a virgin. [Cries again. They all hug again.]

Judy
Did you leave home right after that?

Sita
[Nods] I can't see them again. Ever. I just can't.

Judy
If I treated my children that way, I wouldn't expect them to want a relationship with me. I hurt them with words at times, but I always realized and apologized. I allowed them to confront me.

Naomi
You're my mother, Judy. Do you think you can have another grown kid?

Judy
Absolutely, you are already my daughter. [Judy and Naomi hug.]

Naomi

With you two as my friends, your love and support propels me to the path of healing. You don't make me feel like frayed merchandise.

Sita

You are not frayed, destroyed, damaged or broken. Neither am I, not really. Let's cure ourselves together. How about it, Nurse? [Naomi and Judy laugh.]

Naomi

For the first time, I REALLY feel assured that I WILL heal. It won't be easy. My mind has been programmed like a computer. I've been programmed to think of myself as garbage. I graduated from nursing school near the top of my class, I get promoted every year at the hospital, I invest my money and stay out of debt, and still I feel like shit.

Sita

We've been taught to think of ourselves as untouchables, but we are not! We are strong, beautiful, caring women!

Judy

I second that!

Naomi

I third that, but I have no idea where to start healing from sexual abuse. Do you have any idea, Sita?

Sita

We can first go to the medical library and read everything we can find on overcoming sexual abuse, and find out what has helped other victims. I'm open to the possibility of medication, are you?

[Naomi nods.]

Naomi

I realize there are many things I need to change about my life. I realize Kyle is not right for me. I need to break up with him. I need to do it soon. [Cries]

Judy

I had a hunch you would say something like this. I knew he was wrong for you the first time I saw you two together.

Naomi

Kyle's a great doctor. His patients love him. They swear they couldn't lose weight until he helped them. But he criticizes me unfairly. He would lose his patients if he judged them like he judges me!

Sita

You're doing the right thing. You need to be free.

[They all hug.]

[Lights dim]

<u>Scene 4</u>
A restaurant. Helice looks around nervously. She sips tea from a glass and plays with the salt and pepper shakers. A wait person brings Bertha to the table and hands her a menu.

Helice
I'm so glad you came. I was afraid you wouldn't.

Bertha
Why not?

Helice
After the way I treated you? I'm really sorry.

Bertha
What about the way I treated you? Tearing into you just because you found humor in places where I was blind to it.

Helice
Sometimes I forget that humor can hurt others.

Bertha
Sometimes I forget that many other people cope with humor. Let's respect ourselves no matter what diverse paths to healing we're on. Naomi showed me your poem, "Sex for the Overweight." It's really funny.

Helice
I finally finished it. Lots of truth and dark humor in it, so it was hard to complete. [Pauses] I like the idea that we should respect our separate paths of healing and coping. Really, though, how have you been these past two weeks?

Wait person returns.

Bertha

(To wait person) I'll have the seafood salad and ice tea. No salad dressing and cut the rolls.

Helice

Just dry toast and more tea, please.

Bertha

That's all you're eating?

Helice

For a while, I've been having G.I. issues. This morning it was really bad. But I'm not running fever. Nothing catching. But I asked **you** how you are.

Bertha

I'm concerned about you Helice. Have you seen a doctor?

Helice

I broke down and made an appointment for Tuesday. Tuesday is the soonest the receptionist could fit me in.

Bertha

Have you been getting regular checkups?

Helice

I haven't seen any doc for five years!

Bertha

Before I lost the majority of my weight, I eschewed doctors also.

Helice

My mother believed that physicians had a conspiracy going in order to make more money promoting diets. She swore that all doctors rigged their weight scales up an extra 10 pounds!

Bertha

When my bulimia was really bad and I weighed only 90 pounds, I tried putting paper weights in my pockets, but the nurse noticed the bulges. The truth hurts sometimes.

[*Wait staff serves the food*]

Helice

The truth hurts lots of the time. Did you know Marisa was depressed?

Bertha

She shared her past with me about three years ago. I thought she was okay more recently. She told me what medications worked for her and which did not. Marisa's weight went up and down like mine did. One time we even shared a hot-fudge sundae. When I finally lost 80 pounds, and kept it off, she said I was an inspiration to her. [*Pauses*] She was the only therapist who guided me out of my bulimia. [*Puts down her fork and cries*] I'd rather not talk about Marisa right now.

Helice

[*Takes Bertha's hand*] I wish there was something I could do for you.

Bertha

Just inviting me here and listening to me helps. Back to your G.I. issue – I had lots of them – bulimia always brings them on and when I quit purging and kept on overeating I had them again. You really need to have the symptoms checked out. They may be easily remedied, but they may need some expert treatment.

Helice

I know I'll feel better when I can eat some real food again. I've been eating terribly the last few years. [*Pauses for a few seconds then moans loudly and grabs her abdomen*]

Bertha

I'm calling 911!

Helice

Yes! I've been having these cramps all day!

Bertha

I'm calling 911! (*Grabs her cell phone*)

Next scene. A hospital room. Helice lies in bed smiling radiantly, holding a baby. Bertha, Judy, Naomi and Sita surround the bed.

Helice

Can you believe someone so beautiful came out of me?

Sita

Yes! You are beautiful too, Helice.

Bertha, Judy and Naomi

[*Echoing*] You are beautiful!

Helice

I imagine your babies will be beautiful, Sita, but Caucasian women usually give birth to raw hamburger meat.

Bertha

A typical Helice quip!

Judy

The baby already has a beautiful color, not mottled at all. Lovely lips, lovely nose and hair like silk. [*Strokes the baby's head*]

Naomi

So alert but quiet!

Helice

The pediatrician says she's perfectly healthy! Can you believe it? After all the junk I ate and the beer I drank!

Naomi

There are such things as miracles! And to think of Kyle delivering her! Kyle hasn't delivered a baby since medical school. What a

coincidence he was working in the ER yesterday. This little one
was in a hurry!

Judy
This sweetheart is certainly a miracle. A prize package!

Helice
And I lost 15 pounds instantly. Can you believe I lost 15 pounds
without trying? Must have been because a bariatric doctor
delivered me!

Naomi
I was with you, remember? You pushed really hard. I wouldn't
say you lost the weight effortlessly.

Helice
Not effortlessly, but darn quickly!

[*The women are quiet for a moment.*]

Naomi
Ready for some more good news, Helice: I finally broke up with
Kyle. [*Helice high-fives Naomi.*] We were in the cafeteria
together when the ER beeped us about you.

Helice
I forgive Kyle but only a little! He never should have harassed
you, but he helped me have a beautiful little girl!

Sita
And I broke up with Jeremy. Not that I was ever really with him!

Helice

I knew you would come to your senses! You deserve better than a criminal, even if the criminal is innocent.

Sita
I did not even give him my surname.

Judy
Soon, Sita will feel so good about herself, she'll get herself a real boyfriend.

Bertha
Or she can decide to be single and happy, whatever she wants!

[*The women are silent for a moment.*]

Judy
I admit I'm curious, Helice. But no, it's none of my business!

Helice
Go ahead and ask me whatever you are curious about.

Judy
No, I shouldn't be asking such personal questions.

Helice
I think I know the personal questions on everyone's mind. Since you are all my friends, you deserve to know. Yes, I do know who little Marisa's daddy is – I thinks I will call her Marisa. But I want to tell him first.

Stage directions at the end of *Bertha's Butter Club*:

A knock at the door. A man walks in carrying a huge bouquet of candy bars.

Man

Helice! How are you?

Helice

Allen! How did you find out?

Dyslexic
by Dr. Catherine T. Murray

1

Ronald D. Davis and Eldon M. Braun wrote the book *The Gift of Dyslexia* claiming that dyslexia is a boon rather than a learning disability. Dyslexics often compensate for their symptoms with intuition, emotional intelligence, and creativity. My goal is to accept my own dyslexia as a gift rather than a curse. The idea of a gift or blessing is difficult for me because my symptoms frustrated me and others.

In my early years, until I reached twelve, I experienced undiagnosed dyslexia. Few parents or educators knew about learning disabilities in the 1960s. I skipped words when I read aloud or copied from the blackboard. B's and P's were confused. After I brought home a first grade report card of B's and C's, my harried mother began tutoring me in the evenings. Ironically, at the time, she volunteered as a reading teacher at the town high school. Fortunately, my mother's students responded well to phonics and so did I.

My two first grade teachers both underwent what was previously termed as "nervous breakdowns" shortly before they began a new school year with me and my classmates. Even after the teachers divided the class into two sections, my section was still large with a wide range of student preparedness. Some children did not know the ABC's or other basics while some others could already read. In their frustration the teachers punctuated their words with screams and negative reinforcement. They would angrily tell me, "You don't make sense!" when I read aloud or copied from the board. Classmates learned to bully me and others by overhearing the teachers' blowups.

My confused mother also resorted to angry outbursts. At least once she punished me with a peach tree switch because I was "too stubborn to learn." Other times, she realized I struggled, but she had a hard time believing that reading could challenge me.

Nothing in my early development indicated that I would have learning issues. I talked and formed sentences even earlier than my straight-A older sister had. When Mother read me nursery rhymes and other poetry, I would form rhymes of my own. Mother herself had been a gifted child who had read as a toddler. Again and again she would say, "I don't understand it. You were so smart before you started school."

By the second grade I could read aloud fluently, although I sometimes confused letters and words. Reading comprehension, though, remained a challenge. Even to a certain extent, it remains a challenge today. My mind takes longer than the minds of non-dyslexics to decode words. Focusing on decoding robs the endeavor of comprehension.

Doman Delacato Therapy

Besides the challenges of dyslexic symptoms—the confusion reading textbooks and the extra time it took for studying–the therapy chosen took time and, years later, incurred heartache.

When I was 12, my mother read about a treatment for learning

disabilities called Doman Delacato patterning. It claimed to

rewire the brains of children facing various learning issues. The

developers of the program even claimed to alleviate many

symptoms of serious brain damage such as cerebral palsy.

Glenn Doman, a physical therapist, and Carl Delacato, a reading

specialist, devised the program. The ideology behind the

treatment was developed from an hypothesis of mid-twentieth

century neurosurgeon, Dr. Temple Fay. According to Fay, an

evolutionist, human babies should go through developmental

stages that resemble those of lower animals, or learning issues

would appear later in life. An infant should slide on her thorax

and abdomen like certain reptiles. A few months later, nature

demands that she should creep on four legs like a four-legged

mammal. If a child sits up too soon or walks without going

through the developmental stages of crawling and creeping,

according to Fay, Doman, and Delacato, her brain lacks correct wiring.

Were Fay, Doman, and Delacato correct? Most neurologists and child development experts today condemn the patterning treatment. As far back as 1968 the American Academy of Pediatrics issued a cautionary statement warning parents of the program's pseudoscience.

Yet in 1965 my mother was convinced that the reason why I couldn't always understand what I had read lay in the fact that I had never crawled or crept as a baby. At my first urge to crawl on the floor, she placed me in a baby walker. Even clean floors are dirty places for babies, so she thought that the walker provided a great alternative. When she read about Doman Delacato therapy, she decided to make an appointment for me to be neurologically evaluated.

I felt excited but pessimistic before the evaluation. My self-esteem, at the time, was in the storm drain. I was so afraid the evaluator would tell my mother, "We're sorry, Mrs. Murray, but your daughter's IQ is not high enough for us to help her." Instead, my mother was told that I was "very definitely mixed dominant," which at the time meant early lingo for dyslexic. Mother and I were both told that if I dedicated myself to Doman Delacato therapy, I could bloom academically in a few years. We were promised a cure.

With gusto I proved to be a self-starter regarding my patterning exercises. I was thirsty for knowledge, and I wanted the ability to read and remember what I had read. Applying the perfect coordination that my evaluator taught me, I slid on the floor for about 30 minutes a day and crept on my hands and knees for about 40 minutes each day. The program included several other exercises such as wearing glasses that included a clear red lens over the left eye and placing a clear green sheet over the reading material. The red and green caused my left eye to see only black while my right eye read the material under the clear green plastic.

The explanation regarding this exercise was that my two eyes did

not work as a team. I was training my right eye to dominate the

left eye, so that I would not skip words or confuse letters.

2

Dyslexic 2: Three Years Without Music

As part of my treatment for dyslexia, music was largely

forbidden. The alleged reason behind this severe restriction was

explained as listening to music stimulates the subdominant side of

the brain, and I was trying to strengthen the dominant side of my

brain. This hypothesis has more recently been disproven, but

many dyslexic youth were told to refrain from music in the years

1965 – 1968.

It was allowed for church and for special occasions, but

my evaluators told me that five minutes of music a day would

destroy the effectiveness of a whole hour of neurological

organization (N.O.) exercises. Since I wanted to "get well," and I

worked hard at my N.O., I observed the moratorium on music.

In 1965, when I was 12, I was looking forward to my

fourth year of taking piano and my first full year of playing the *Glockenspiel.* Music constituted a major part of my life. Besides playing music, I loved listening to show tunes, especially Julie Andrews and Mary Martin. Moreover, the years 1965 – 1968 exploded with rock music innovation. My peers were always talking about their favorite groups and who they were listening to on their transistors. Adolescents communicate with music lyrics, but I was deaf to their language. Needless to say, the no-music years were lonely years for me. I remember riding my bicycle to the end of a block and watching a school bus pass full of the school band. When my class went to choir, I stayed in a study hall.

Despite the solitariness, though, I survived. I wrote my first story and continued writing poems. In the quietude I read more. Did the neurological organization exercises cure me? No, but I received a powerful placebo effect for several years. In 1968 my parents generally considered me "cured." I began boarding school, and creeping, crawling, and a restriction of music would have been impractical. By the end of my sophomore year of high

school, I earned the honor roll.

3

Taking the SAT exams caused great frustration. In the early 1970's test proctors did not observe special accommodations for learning disabled students. Since I read slowly and was easily distracted, I simply didn't have enough time to determine the correct answers. My first college choice, the University of Dallas, turned me down because of my poor SAT scores. Ironically, U.D. would later accept me for graduate school.

Austin College accepted me for my bachelor's degree, and I entered the liberal arts school in the spring of 1971. The academic demands gave me the painful conclusion that my reading and concentrating challenges were not cured, and perhaps the Doman-Delacato patterning program only boosted me psychologically for a temporary period.

Feeling duped, I became depressed.

I sought professional help and became even more dispirited in the process. The clinical psychologist knew nothing about dyslexia and insisted on giving me an IQ test when I could barely hold a pencil.

My parents could not understand why a former high school honor student would struggle in college. Their answer to my depression was "Snap out of it. You're one of the lucky ones." True, I was grateful to attend college, but I was overwhelmed with reading 80 pages a day.

Sadly, I'm certain my father also suffered from dyslexia. Although he graduated from high school, and later became a realtor, he had failed an elementary or junior high grade. If he had been open about his own challenges, he could have been an ideal role model for me. Instead, he practiced denial for both of us.

In desperation, I again tried the Doman-Delacato patterning program. In the summer of 1971, I entered the University of

Plano, a tiny college and secondary school specializing in neurological organization treatment. Not all the students at U.P. needed this treatment, but those that did often felt disheartened by its lack of success.

I reentered Austin College in the spring of 1973 determined to make my efforts a success. Deciding that no outside person or therapy could help my reading comprehension, I buckled down by my junior year to pull up my GPA. I graduated in 1975 with a BA in English.

4

It took me many years to realize that everyone has challenges in life, and dyslexia is my main challenge. It slows my reading and concentration down, but it does not prevent me from learning. Identifying as a victim kept me from performing adequately. Once I learned to appreciate the gifts that God constantly gives me, I learned to succeed.

In the fall of 1977 I entered the University of Dallas to begin a degree in creative writing. I had written my first poem at eight, and my first story at 12. Despite my experience in creative writing, my mentor, novelist Caroline Gordon, decided that all her students needed to be well grounded in the classics before we showed her any of our writing.

At Austin College I had mostly studied modern literature. Mythology had been read only in bits and pieces, so I dove into Homer, Sophocles, Euripides, Aeschylus, Dante and others. I had almost no time for friends or family. Not long after finishing the course work for the MA, I was hospitalized for depression. Separation from support systems affected my psyche, but what really caused my psychological state was my anger and despair.

I've learned to appreciate the knowledge gained at the University of Dallas, but 40 years ago I was annoyed and bitter over the long hours of reading to achieve what classmates could do in half the time. If I had not been so angry and resentful, I would have focused on my writing and finished the degree earlier. Remember Aesop's fable of the tortoise and the hare? I was the tortoise who got even more behind because I stopped and complained along the way.

Emotional intelligence and wisdom constitute more value than the knowledge gained in degrees. Gradually, I let go of my hostility and jealousy of others who seemed to achieve easily. I began to empathize with them and learn as a team player.

Besides understanding and awareness, I have also discovered gratefulness. For the last ten years, I have been thankful to work in my field. English majors are not the most prized in the job market, and they haven't been for almost 50 years. I now have a PhD, and I discovered that college positions in liberal arts fields are few. It took me awhile, but I finally landed a position in a community college. Today, I love what I do, teaching composition and literature.

Susan Atkins and Karla Faye Tucker

Susan Atkins and Karla Faye Tucker were both convicted of brutal, seemingly senseless murders, Atkins in California and Tucker in Texas. Atkins and Tucker butchered their victims while high on speed, a known inducer of violence. Probably to sound tough and scary, the attractive brunettes later bragged that they experienced sexual gratification from stabbing and jabbing their victims. They had both worked in sexually exploitive professions, Susan as a topless dancer and Karla Faye as a prostitute. Each spent time on Death Row. Atkins' death sentence was overturned in 1972, yet she was still in prison when she died from cancer in 2009. Tucker was executed in 1998. The two women allegedly converted to Christianity from behind bars like many other prisoners. Only God understands a human's heart, but Karla Faye's faith seems more believable than Susan's.

Atkins' account of her role in the Manson murders kept changing. While in jail for her assistance in another murder, she boasted to two cellmates that every time Sharon Tate screamed she stabbed the actress again. By the time Susan testified under oath before a Grand Jury, her story modified her personal guilt. At the same time, her words, voice, and demeanor revealed little or no remorse. She still admired cult leader Charles Manson. Altering her earlier account cost Susan immunity from the death penalty. With her codefendants, Susan disrupted the legal process during her long trial. One day she lunged toward a display knife and was promptly handcuffed by bailiffs. Atkins omits her courtroom antics in two books she published after her supposed Christian conversion.

In contrast to Atkins, Tucker stated she wanted to "come clean." At her trial, her only defense was her altered drug state when she broke and entered Jerry Lynn Dean's apartment in order to rob motorcycle parts. Surprised to find people present, Karla

Faye angrily grabbed a pickax (from outside the apartment) and hacked to death Dean and his female companion, Deborah Thornton. Earlier, Dean had deliberately destroyed a photo of Karla Faye's late mother and had accidentally ruined her carpet by placing an oil dripping motorcycle in her home.

Tucker knew one of her victims, Dean, and the other, Thornton, was killed to prevent reporting. Atkins knew only one of her six victims, musician Gary Hinman. Even if Susan Atkins did not stab any of the victims, as she later maintained, she did admit to restraining the victims, enabling their horrific deaths. Stabbing with a knife and lancing with a pickax both constitute personal attacks. The extreme rage that Atkins and Tucker demonstrated likely came, at least in part, from projection— Charles Manson had instructed Susan to kill the pigs, the wealthy people who preyed on the poor. Although Karla Faye was irate over her mother's photo and ruined carpet, perhaps her extreme

acrimony came from years of abuse.

Both Susan Atkins and Karla Tucker came from troubled,

neglectful families. Atkins' alcohol abusing mother came down

with cancer and died when Susan was in her teens. The distressed

girl then attempted to take on domestic responsibilities with no

help from her father and brothers. She soon left home. Tucker's

mother also passed away when Karla Faye was in her teens, but

not before she had introduced her youngest daughter to drugs and

prostitution. While their exploitation and their apparent drug

addiction do not excuse Atkins and Tucker from the crimes they

committed, a glance into their girlhood emits some understanding

about the anger that led to murder.

After four years of incarceration, Susan Atkins stated that

she had repented of her sins and accepted Jesus Christ as her

Savior and Lord. Perhaps she did. I hope she did. But after numerous parole hearings failed to free her, Susan Atkins

attempted to sue the state of California for *habeas corpus*.

Karla Faye Tucker also sobered and began reading the

Bible in jail. Unlike Atkins, though, Tucker did not demand

leadership due to her newfound faith. Her guidance for others

came from Karla Faye's gentleness, wisdom, and humility. All of

her earlier bitterness was gone as she planned light-hearted,

healing activities for the other women on death row.

When Tucker ran out of appeals, after 14 years on Death

Row, many people including conservatives Pat Robertson and

Newt Gingrich opposed the State of Texas' plan to execute Karla

Faye. Even some of the prison authorities saw the change in the

young woman who behind bars had married a prison chaplain,

Dana Lane Brown.

But then-governor George W. Bush refused to grant

clemency to Tucker and allow her to serve life in prison instead of

receiving death. The state of Texas executed Karla Faye Tucker of February 3, 1998 leaving behind millions of grievers from her

fellow inmates on Death Row to everyday Christians in family

churches.

Two Preventable Deaths

In the fall of 1977, two Texas women died from ill-done abortions, leaving a total of six children motherless. Abortion rights groups exploited the illegal abortion death of Rosaura Jimenez into a highly-publicized, cause-celeb. Yet, the same pro-choice activists remained silent about the legal, but equally horrific, abortion death of Louchrisser Jackson.

Many editorialists blamed Rosaura "Rosie" Jimenez's death on Congressman Henry Hyde, who had authored the Hyde Amendment which discontinued federal funds for Medicaid abortions. Ms. Jimenez had already undergone two Medicaid-funded abortions when her physician informed her that funds had been cut off for another procedure that she sought. Rosie then acquired a termination from an unlicensed midwife who charged her $120 to insert a catheter into her cervix. The 27-year-old soon experienced septic shock and gangrene. She was admitted to

McAllen General Hospital and died from renal and cardiac failure on October 3, 1977.

Louchrisser Jackson's legal abortion death occurred only a month after Rosie Jimenez's death. Ms. Jackson terminated her 12-week pregnancy at Reproductive Services, formerly on Inwood Road in Dallas. A vacuum aspirator, in the hands of Dr. Gardiner, M.D., left the mother of five with a severely perforated uterus. Louchrisser lost nearly two liters of blood.

Despite the proximity of Reproductive Services to Parkland Hospital and its extensive emergency services and blood bank, Dr. Gardiner ordered blood to be delivered to Reproductive Services. Like many abortion clinic personnel, the inept physician feared that an emergency ambulance would attract negative publicity to the facility, so only a lesser-equipped, slower private ambulance was called.

Louchrisser Jackson, whose life probably could have been spared, died of cardiac arrest shortly after Dr. Gardiner, frustrated over the delay of the blood shipment, took blood from his own body and transfused it into his patient. Sadly, Dr. Gardiner's blood was Type B and Ms. Jackson's was an incompatible Type O.

When the 23-year-old ultimately arrived at a hospital, Dr. Gardiner instructed the emergency physician to falsify his report so that neither Gardiner nor Reproductive Services would be blamed for the fatality. The emergency doctor refused. Nevertheless, Louchrisser Jackson's heartbreaking death went under-reported until the following year when another patient of Dr. Gardiner's sued Reproductive Services for negligence. Fortunately, the plaintiff lived but only after suffering a severed uterine artery and undergoing shock, blood transfusions, and a hysterectomy.

Despite the nationwide headlines that reported Rosie Jimenez's untimely death, pro-choice groups remained hushed about the two known botched procedures at Dallas' Reproductive

Services. Organizations, such as The National Abortion Rights Action League, almost always remain silent about victims of legal terminations. Abortion, whether it is illegal or legal, is not necessarily a safe procedure.

Do pro-choice groups truly care about women seeking to terminate their pregnancies? Perhaps certain members of abortion rights organizations care deeply about women and their health and welfare. But collectively, abortion rights committees appear to sometimes abandon the very women on which their organizations focus. Louchrisser Jackson, like Rosie Jimenez, was a poor minority woman. In spite of the enormous publicity surrounding victims of illegal abortions, pro-choice groups seldom report similar abuses in licensed clinics. If they truly care about Rosie, they would also care about Louchrisser.

CCTE Conference

5 October 2019

Abstract:"Identity and Rhetorical Presence in Caroline Gordon's 'The Petrified Woman'"

Sally seeks identity with her late mother's relatives in Caroline Gordon's short story, "The Petrified Woman". The Southern Gothic story takes place in the early years of the twentieth century. Sally considers herself an outsider, so she seeks connection at Cousin Tom's estate and plays with Tom's daughter, Hilda. The Fork (where two creeks flow together) and nearby Arthur's Cave, where an enormous family reunion takes place, provide rhetorical presence between the past and the present. For generations, Sally's mother's extended family has owned adjoining rural Kentucky property. The Fork symbolizes marriage, and the maternal family had intermarried for many years in order to hold on to the land. The sound of the creeks' waters and the music of a mockingbird delight Sally. She admires Cousin Tom's new wife who disdains the mockingbird and the surrounding nature. Like Sally's father, the bride voices sarcastic remarks about the coming family reunion. At the reunion the unsupervised Sally, Hilda, and a third cousin comically overeat and attend an outside freak show with a drunken Cousin Tom. Cousin Tom's fascination with the allegedly petrified woman causes the breakup of his marriage. At home at the dinner table, with a dozen relatives in attendance, he announces he is in love with the petrified woman. As he leaves to seek the woman, he trips and falls. At the end of the story, Sally relates that her two cousins had divorced each other and had remarried. The property had burned down, probably because of Cousin Tom's alcoholic carelessness. Sally hints at sadness but not jadedness from her once admired relatives' destroyed union.

Rhetorical Presence of The Fork and "The Petrified Woman"

Cate Murray

Literary Submission for CCTE Conference

12 February 2020

Cate Murray

CCTE Conference

12 February 2020

Rhetorical Presence of The Fork and "The Petrified
Woman"

The Agrarian Movement provides the tone of

Caroline Gordon's fiction as upholding nature and family

farms over a concrete and steel urban life and less

meaningful professions. Gordon was the wife of Allen Tate, who helped found the Agrarian Movement, and she shared Tate's philosophy that rural life among natural settings, family bonds, and tradition tends to enrich humans spiritually. Separating oneself from nature, whether physically or emotionally, inclines humans toward spiritual devastation. Juxtaposing the natural and nurturing with the artificial and annihilating, Caroline Gordon illustrates a subconscious choice of the narrator, Sally Maury, in "The Petrified Woman." In the resolution Sally identifies more with tradition and nature than with rebellion and superficiality.

Gordon sets the Southern Gothic story in southeastern Kentucky near the Tennessee line in the early years of the twentieth century. Sally visits Cousin Tom and Cousin Eleanor at their homestead, The Fork, where two creeks flow together. The rhetorical presence of The

Fork and its soothing effect contrasts with the petrified

woman, who appears later in the story, and her disturbing

influence on Sally's Cousin Tom.

The two creeks joined together represent marriage

and tradition. Sally's maternal family has lived on and

worked on the surrounding land for generations. Robert

Penn Warren describes the area as "a section of

considerable Revolutionary grant land, chopped up,

generation by generation, despite the device of cousinly

marriages" (vii). Since so many of the kin are double

cousins, Sally and the other children in the story address

adult relatives with the title of "cousin." Sally considers

herself "peculiar" because her mother had married outside

the connection and because she attends a boys' school

instead of a girls' school (6).

Sally believes that the massive family reunion to

be held in Arthur's Cave where "we expected all our kin

and connections to come, some as far off as California"

(3) will give her a chance to more fully belong to her

mother's family. After playing in the creeks all day with

Cousin Tom's daughter, Hilda, Sally and her young cousin

talk excitedly about the reunion the next day. Despite the

girls' enthusiasm, Hilda's new stepmother, Cousin

Eleanor, expresses disdain for the event. "Five hundred

people repairing en masse to the womb [Arthur's Cave]--

what a sight it must be" (4).

Almost oblivious to Cousin Eleanor's sarcasm,

Sally delights in hearing "the creek running over the

rocks" and Eleanor's white dress brush against the floor as

she swings in the porch swing. In the girl's mind, her new

cousin's music of her skirt and the prenatal sound of the

flowing water on the rocks are both part of The Fork—a

place of tradition and nurturing. According to Sally,

Cousin Tom's bride is "the prettiest person ever lived"

although Sally's grandmother "said she didn't like her mouth" (4).

Like Sally's father, Professor Aleck Maury, Cousin Eleanor is also an outsider to the family connections. Neither understand the bonds of family or tradition. Before she left for The Fork, Sally heard her schoolmaster father criticize the planned reunion. "All those mediocre people, getting together to congratulate themselves on their mediocrity! I ain't taking a step." When Sally surprisingly sees her father at the reunion, she reasons, "he likes to see them making fools of themselves" (6).

Professor Maury particularly mocks the speech of Cousin Robert D. Owen Fayerlee, the wealthy kin who had chartered Arthur's Cave and donated five cases of whiskey for the 500 relatives. "He said that the Fayerlees were descended from Edward the Confessor and Philippe le Bel of France and the grandfather of George

Washington" (7). Professor Maury reacts to the speech by exclaiming, "Now ain't that tooting?" (8) Cousin Edward Barker agrees with Maury. "The Fayerlees have been plain, honest countrymen since 1600. Don't that fool know anything about his own family?" (8)

The apparent dishonesty of Cousin Robert D. Owen Fayerlee's speech denotes the breakdown of family and tradition. Even though the cousin has become wealthy in St. Louis, he seeks to further impress his relatives by embellishing the roots of his side of the family and engender a false pride to the Fayerlee branch. He is the self-appointed clan storyteller, but his audience ridicules him instead of listening to him. Universally, the carrying down of generational stories generates family pride, but Cousin Robert D. Fayerlee only produces more of his own hubris. Also, the liquor that Fayerlee has donated "so everyone will have a good time" (5) serves to diminish the joy of the reunion for many relatives.

Even before the huge lunch Sally, Hilda, and another young relative named Susie notice that Cousin Tom smells like liquor and mistakes Sally for his own daughter. As the women set up the noon meal Tom "knocked into a lady and when he stepped back he ran into another one, so after he asked them to excuse him he went off on tiptoe. But he lifted his feet too high and put one of them down into a basket of pies" (7). His wife, Cousin Eleanor, looks at him without saying anything.

In spite of the disturbing alcohol-fueled follies of Cousin Tom, the three unsupervised girls manage to comically overeat causing Hilda a stomach ache. When Hilda's pain subsides, the girls leave Arthur's Cave and encounter Cousin Giles Allard "who is not quite right in the head." The girls try to dismiss Cousin Giles but he follows the girls to meet Cousin Tom. In a jolly mood

Cousin Tom gives the girls money, and the five of them

decide to attend the nearby carnival. The overpriced

carnival consists of a one-wagon, poorly performed freak

show. The barker shouts, "Stell-a, Stell-a, the One and

Only Stell-a!/ Not flesh, not bone,/ But calkypyrate stone,

/ Sweet Sixteen a Hundred Years Ago / And Sweet

Sixteen Today!" (9)

The reclining "Sweet Sixteen" girl wears "a white

satin dress. It was cut so low that you could see her

bosom." When "Cousin Giles Allard squeaked like a

rabbit" the girl opens her eyes and breathes noticeably.

The show soon ends, and Cousin Tom over tips the barker.

Tom remarks, "She's a pretty woman. I don't know when

I've seen a prettier woman...lies quiet, too..." (10).

Giles, Hilda, and Susie want to stay and determine

how the petrified woman can breathe if she's been dead

for a century. But the girls apparently perceive a need to

chaperon the intoxicated adult, Cousin Tom, who wanders

back toward the cave. Tom, who apparently does not

realize how much his mind is altered by alcohol, expresses

concern for the petrified woman. He shouts at Cousin

Giles Allard "the way he hollers at the hands on the place"

because he doesn't want "him snooping around Stella."He

tells the girls, "Maybe she isn't dead. Maybe she is just

resting" (11).

Hilda dreads her new stepmother's reaction when

Cousin Eleanor encounters Cousin Tom's severe

drunkenness. "It just drives her crazy when he drinks," she

tells Sally and Susie, but Susie states, "She better get used

to it. All the Fayerlee men drink" (12). Susie's statement

about "all the Fayerlee men," and her apparent acceptance

of Cousin Tom's extreme intoxication, indicates that

alcohol abuse may be too common among Sally's kin and

connections. The tradition of kinsmen drinking together has apparently sullied into an unhealthy tradition. At least one relative, Cousin Tom, drinks alone and largely avoids his kin and connections at the reunion.

Back home at The Fork, Cousin Eleanor tells Cousin Marie, "Wine for dinner. We don't need it. There's no use for us to deny ourselves just because Tom can't control himself" (13). Cousin Eleanor, who may not realize she is enabling her husband's addiction, is dressed more like a *femme fatale* than a recent bride. Sally says, "I will never forget the dress she had on that night. It was black but thin and it had a rose-colored bow right on the hip" (13). Earlier, she had worn a white dress.

At the dinner table, surrounded by about a dozen relatives, Sally and Hilda play a petrified woman game that they secretly devised. As usual, most of the adults ignore the two girls until Cousin Tom overhears them talking about the "Sweet Sixteen." Cousin Tom shuts his eyes and tells everyone present about the woman with "real charm." Cousin Eleanor asks him why she is charming, and he tells her that she is charming because she is petrified. "Some women are just petrified in spots. She was petrified all over" (14).

Sally states, "I looked at her and then I wished I hadn't. She had blue eyes. I always thought that they were like violets. She had a way of opening them wide whenever she looked at you...It was like the violets were freezing, there in her eyes" (14). Sally fears Cousin Eleanor will freeze Cousin Tom with her eyes, but he seemed to relish her defiance, for a few seconds.

Spousal substance abuse and her own disgust turn Cousin Eleanor from a bride in a white dress to an Ice Queen, akin to C.S. Lewis's Jadis who freezes Narnia for a century. Her anger turns her into another type of petrified woman, one that does not lay still. Unlike the allegedly ossified woman, Cousin Eleanor has the power to petrify or frighten others.

Cousin Tom continues about the petrified woman at the carnival, "She just lay there and looked sweet. I like a woman to look sweet...Hell, they ain't got anything else to do!" (14). He states, "I'm going down to Arthur's Cave and take her away from that fellow" (15).

Cousin Tom does not move far. He gets up from the table but accidentally catches his foot on Cousin Marie's dress. He falls, breaks his wine glass, and cuts his forehead before he can complete his chivalrous quest.

Sally relates that her two cousins divorced and The Fork burned down, perhaps because a drunken Tom was careless with a lighted lamp. Although she never again attends another family reunion, she still thinks of Cousin Eleanor wearing a white dress, not the thin black dress with the red bow at the hip. Tom, though, is still on the floor in Sally's mind. As Veronica A. Makowsky explains, "Eleanor is associated with the revivifying and cleansing properties of water...and Tom is petrified in his self destruction" (184). Although the angry Ice Queen moves away from The Fork and its "revivifying and cleansing properties," Sally, the protagonist, views her beloved relative in a more wholesome light and becomes less jaded by Cousin Tom's alcohol abuse and her cousins' marital discord.

Sources

Gordon, Caroline. "The Petrified Woman."

Caroline Gordon: The Collected Stories.

Nashville: J.S. Sanders, 1981.

Makowsky, Veronica A. *Caroline Gordon: A*

Biography. New York: Oxford UP, 1989.

Warren, Robert Penn. "Introduction." *Caroline*

Gordon: The Collected Stories. Nashville:

J.S. Sanders, 1981.

Out of the Mouths of Babes

A One-Act Play by Cate Murray

Characters:

Veronica Fleming – The verbose 13 year old daughter of a divorced physician and a law student. Veronica attends a Christian school and is active on the debate team. For someone her age, she is very knowledgeable about life issues including fetology.

Dr. Hank Fleming – Veronica's father who has recently completed his residency in emergency medicine. He works long hours at more than one medical position to pay back medical school loans and to overcompensate for perceived financial neglect of Veronica.

Dr. Paige Simmons – Dr. Fleming's girlfriend and the owner of the Baker Street Women's Clinic where Hank Fleming works.

Friedan Simmons – Dr. Simmons' 17 year old daughter who was conceived by an anonymous donor and in-vitro fertilization. She works as receptionist at her mother's clinic.

Kayley – A battered young woman who is a patient at the Baker Street Women's Clinic.

Mrs. Gillespie – Veronica's debate coach.

Priscilla Hogan – A nurse at the clinic. She tries to overdose after assisting with a late-term abortion.

Customers in an ice cream parlor.

Pro-life sidewalk counselors.

A uniformed police officer.

Two psych ward attendants.

<u>*Act 1, Scene 1*</u>
[*Lights*]

Hank shows Veronica her new room in his luxury condo.

Veronica

[*Ecstatic*] Oh Daddy, it's beautiful! I can't believe that you remembered that I always wanted a blue and white room with white poodle décor!

Hank

You told me enough times when you were little.

Veronica

I probably bugged you about it. [*Picks up a stuffed poodle and feels of its hair*]

Hank

Don't worry. Now I can make all your dreams come true. My boss, Dr. Paige Simmons, has a friend who owns a quilt shop. The proprietor helped me pick out this pattern and the material.

Veronica

But I bet you put together the other stuff. I didn't think a man could decorate like this!

Hank

Men trained in surgery do have an artistic flair.

Veronica

Well you certainly do. Really, I love this room! [*She picks up a framed photo.*] Don't tell me this is Louie.

Hank

Yep, your Granny's obnoxious little white poodle!

Veronica

Remember when Louie used to bare his crooked teeth at you whenever you came near Granny or me?

Hank

I'm afraid so.

Veronica

He hated men and boys, but he loved most women, especially Granny. [*Pauses*] I really miss her.

Hank

I miss her too. I always knew what was on her mind because she would tell me. [*Pauses*] Whether I wanted to hear it or not. You sort of have the same trait, but I'm telling you this as a compliment.

Veronica

Remember when I kept having cravings for Heath Bars, and Granny would say [*Veronica and Hank in union*] "Heath Bars are not health bars! You are eating pimples and fat!" [*Veronica only*] But remember Granny's health bars? They tasted like yucky vitamin pills, and they probably contained more sugar than Heath Bars.

Hank

They do contain *more* sugar as well as more fat. But Mom swore by them because they contain 15 grams of protein and bee pollen. [*Laughs*] They're made for people who run or work out for hours at a time. [*Dinner bell rings*]

Veronica

Speaking of food… [*They leave for the dining room.*]

Hank

I've been salivating over that tomato and oregano aroma!
*Hank and Veronica sit at the table. Veronica butters a piece of
bread while Hank takes a bite of the lasagna, shows surprise at
biting a hard chunk, then discreetly takes a piece from his mouth
onto a paper napkin.*

Hank

Honey, how long did you boil the pasta?

Veronica

Boil the pasta? I baked it. [*She bites into a piece and also
experiences a chunk. She swallows with a large gulp of milk.*]
Great Grandma Del `Osso's recipe said nothing about boiling the
pasta before putting it in the lasagna!

Hank

Since she was Italian, she wrote the recipe assuming that
everyone would boil the pasta first. Actually, lots of people don't
know that.

Veronica

But I wanted to make something special for you!

Hank

You're here. That's special enough for me!

Veronica

But I wanted your grandma's recipe to be perfect.

Hank

[*Picks the pasta out of the casserole dish and places it on a dessert plate.*] Look, we'll have a delicious dinner with fewer carbs – bread provides enough carbs anyway – and we'll call it tomato-ricotta-zucchini casserole. And there's plenty of this wonderful salad – homegrown tomatoes and Lebanese olives!

Veronica

Next time I'll triple check the recipe!

Hank

Sure you will. I have great faith in you as a cook. When I first met your mother, I used to use ketchup as spaghetti sauce!

Veronica

Mom tells me that she wasn't such a great cook either.

Hank

She never had a chance. We were too broke to buy many spices. We moved one time and we let a friend pack our kitchen stuff. He packed the spices in an open box that fell off the truck into the street! [*Pauses*] But let's change the subject. I want to hear about you and the debate team.

Veronica

I was really scared the other day, but everything turned out great. On short notice Mrs. Gillespie told me to research the personhood of the fetus so that I could defend the pro-life side in a debate. Mrs. Gillespie herself played the devil's advocate and pretended to be pro-abortion.

Hank

You'll become a scientist yet.

Veronica

I'm hoping to combine your scientific abilities and mom's legal aptitude and become a Constitutional attorney. I'll help overthrow Roe vs. Wade unless it is already abolished by the time I finish school.

Hank

Tell me how your teacher defended pro-choice.

Veronica

The usual stuff. The same worn-out rhetoric. Women's rights – never mind about the babies' rights. What if the women were raped.

Hank

What *if* the woman was raped?

Veronica

Studies show that rape victims often suffer more from abortion than women who were not raped. And sometimes the woman psychologically experiences the rape again during the abortion. Besides, should an innocent little baby take the death penalty for the father's crime?

Hank

Honey, sometimes so-called scientific studies are skewed for a certain outcome.

Veronica

[*Quickly and excitedly*] You bet they are! In the 1960s, the National Association for the Repeal of Abortion Laws (now The National Abortion Rights Action League) published that over 100,000 illegal abortions were performed every year and women were dying from them. There were never that many illegal abortions performed in the United States, and many, many more women die from *legal* abortions now!

Hank

Let's talk about something more pleasant.

Veronica

Are you sure you are getting enough to eat?

Hank

Sure, this salad is great. I'm getting enough meat and cheese from the lasagna. Really, I don't need the carbs from the pasta.

[*Doorbell rings*]

Hank

I'll get the door. [*Hank opens the door, and Dr. Paige Simmons and her daughter, Friedan, stand in the doorway.*] Come on in! Paige and Friedan, meet my one and only daughter, Veronica.

Paige

Don't I smell oregano? Hank, I thought you signed an agreement that you wouldn't smoke oregano while you worked for me.

[*All laugh.*]

Veronica

How do you do, Dr. Simmons, Frieda?

Paige

My, aren't you the formal one! Since you're Hank's daughter you can call me Paige. And my daughter isn't Frieda. Her name is Friedan after the writer, Betty Friedan. Maybe you and Friedan

can get together while you're here. Why don't you show her your
new room?

Veronica

You mean Betty Friedan of that 1960s book, *The Feminine
Mystique?*

Paige

The very same!

Veronica

Did you know that Betty Friedan also founded the National
Association for the Repeal of Abortion Laws? She's responsible
for the deaths of over sixty-million babies!

Hank

Veronica's on the debate team at her school. She knows
everything!

Veronica

Not everything, Daddy! You two doctors know a lot more.

Hank

Yes, Dear. Paige and I have some clinic business to discuss.

Veronica

Sure, Dad.

[*Friedan stares at her mom and Hank as she follows Veronica
into her room.*]

Paige

[*Places her arms around Hank*] I finally get you alone. It's been a whole week since we've been alone! The clinic's been Grand Central lately, but think of the money!

Hank

[*Pulls away from Paige*] Paige, Veronica doesn't know about the clinic – that we perform abortions.

Paige

That's obvious. And we agreed to refer to the procedures as legal services because that's what they are! Remember?

Hank

I'm worried about Veronica or her mom finding out about these legal services. Veronica attends a Christian school, and she's on the debate team. She constantly spouts off statistics supporting pro-life issues.

Paige

And you pay for that crappy education?

Hank

Bethany Academy is a great school academically. She'll get into a good college. The main thing is that she's happy there.

Paige

But she doesn't know how you're building her college fund!

Hank

Please Paige, I want to keep it that way.

Paige

How long is she visiting?

Hank

Just for another week. Her school starts again soon. And I'll miss her terribly when she goes.

Paige

I'll lend you Friedan! Now that she's earning her own money and driving her own car, she stays away with her friends most of the time.

Hank

Don't you miss having her around more often?

Paige

I don't miss her snide remarks. She seems to think I can't do anything right anymore!

Hank

Does Friedan know about us? I haven't told Veronica yet.

Paige

Of course Friedan knows! And she likes you. Why do you want to keep Veronica in the dark about everything?

Hank

I think Veronica wants her mom and me to get back together.

Paige

Do you still love Robin?

Hank

Part of me will always love Robin. I couldn't have picked a better mother for my daughter. But I screwed up the relationship. When the road got bumpy, I concentrated excessively on my studies, and I fell for the attentions of some female classmates.

Paige

We all make mistakes, but you sure as hell better not be chasing cute, young medical students now! [*Pulls him towards her and kisses him*]

[*Friedan and Veronica enter the room. Friedan smirks.*]

Friedan

[*Facetiously*] What cute, young medical students?

Paige

Well I guess we're not so alone at all. [*Paige, Hank, and Friedan all laugh. Veronica looks puzzled.*]

<u>*Act 1, Scene 2*</u>

Veronica and Friedan sit at a table in a retro ice cream shop enjoying sundaes. Vintage advertisements hang in the background. Retro music plays.

Veronica

I love this place, especially the metal signs.

Friedan

I come here for the real ice cream. The décor sort of reminds me of your room [*laughs*].

Veronica

Friedan, I realize that you like things other than sentimental signs and white poodles, but I think you're communicating not just diversity but hostility toward me.

Friedan

I'm not hostile, but a white poodle quilt is awfully funny. While you're psychoanalyzing me, I'm psychoanalyizing you. I hear that you're drawn to white poodles because your grandmother had one.

Veronica

That's right.

Friedan

Funny. My mother's mother had a cat, but I certainly wouldn't want a cat quilt.

Veronica

In debate, we learn how to detect possible opposition from the audience member's body language, questions, and comments. I perceive some unfriendliness from both your mom and you.

Friedan

Again, I'm not hostile and neither is Mom. We're just strong women with opinions, and you've got your opinions too. If we end up in the same family, we'll have to have separate bedrooms, but with the amount my mom makes and your dad makes, extra bedrooms shouldn't be a problem.

Veronica

[*Put down her spoon quickly*] They're not thinking of getting married, are they?

Friedan

If they are, it'll be a quick civil affair. Mom hates traditional weddings. They might live together first.

Veronica

Dad would never do that!

Friedan

Everybody co-habitates these days! How do you think couples get to know each other?

Veronica

Lots of people don't! The Bible teaches that fornication is a sin. Dad says that he believes in the Bible.

Friedan

Let me see your ring. [*Veronica takes off her ring and hands it to Friedan. The older girl reads the inscription.*] "True love waits." I thought you might have one of these rings.

Veronica

True love really does wait until marriage.

Friedan

Hank would say anything to make you happy. Maybe you could even talk him out of moving in with Mom. But some mornings I hear him slip out before dawn. [*Pauses and looks at Veronica's face*] Seriously, I think your closeness with your dad is sweet. [*Pauses*] I never knew my dad at all. He was just a sperm donor.

Veronica

It sounds like you had a difficult relationship with your father. But you shouldn't refer to him as "just a sperm donor."

Friedan

Why not? That's what he was or is. Appeared at a fertility clinic, jacked off into a container, the sperm was implanted into Mom, and I'm the result! Mom never even met him. All I know about him is that he was a medical student and he had some traits that Mom preferred.

Veronica

Don't you want to find him, get to know him?

Friedan

Why? He probably has about 75 kids by now. Maybe 275! [Laughs]

Veronica

I can't imagine having so many brothers and sisters or even the possibility of it. I'd want to meet all of them.

Friedan

You're strange.

Veronica

Thank you.

Friedan

Why are you thanking me?

Veronica

I'm care about human life. I'm glad you're here even though I don't believe in artificial insemination. If concerns for other humans make me strange, so be it.

Friedan

Without artificial insemination, the only way to have a baby is sex, and you don't like that either.

Veronica

Nothing is wrong with sex between a loving married couple. Sex is a gift from God.

Friedan

Are fetuses a gift from God?

Veronica

Absolutely!

Friedan

What's it like to be friends with fetuses?

Veronica

[*Pauses and looks into Paige's eyes*] We all came from fertilized eggs. Can *you* make a fertilized egg by yourself?

Friedan

I can't even make an omelette. But I know lots of feminists who are great cooks…

Veronica

Don't change the subject! A fertilized egg has 46 chromosomes and the blueprint for a unique human being. Only God can make a human being.

Friedan

[*Claps*] What do you think about your dad terminating fertilized cells and embryos?

Veronica

But he doesn't. He wouldn't. He's an emergency care physician. He saves lives. He doesn't destroy them!

Friedan

Sure, he works in the ER during the week, but he relieves the troubles of women at the Baker Street Women's Clinic on most weekends. He and mom both love the quick cash they make. Hank wants to pay off his med school loans and send you off to college in style!

Veronica

You're lying! Dad would never perform abortions!

Friedan smirks at Veronica. They are both silent for a moment.

Veronica

You wouldn't kid about this?

[*Friedan shakes her head.*]

Veronica

It's not like him. He's so loving. [*Covers her face with a napkin and cries*]

Friedan

Of course he loves you. Look at all the money he spends on you!

Veronica

I don't want the money or the nice things if it comes from killing babies! [*Other customers look at Veronica.*]

Friedan

You're making a scene here! I suppose you think I'm a baby killer too since I work as a receptionist at the clinic.

Veronica

Yes! [*Quickly lays down a couple of bills and starts to leave the ice cream parlor*]

Friedan

Hey! How are you going to get back to your Dad's? [*Veronica glares at Friedan and runs out.*] Suit yourself!

Act 1, Scene 3

Baker Street Women's Clinic. Paige walks into an examination room and greets a patient named Kayley.

Paige

Hello, Kayley. I'm Dr. Simmons, the director of the clinic. [*Shakes her hand*] How are you today?

Kayley

Fine.

Paige

Dr. Brown wanted me to talk to you because you're at 15 weeks gestation. At this clinic, we generally perform services at 13 weeks and under.

Kayley

I've got to have an abortion today. I've got to!

[*Paige gets a good look at Kayley and looks concerned.*]

Paige

You realize that the fee will be $850 instead of $500? We have to take extra time and care with more advanced pregnancies.

Kayley

I figured it would cost more than it did last time. I've got the money.

Paige

[*Pauses and looks at Kayley*] You've got a bruise on your face. Who gave that to you?

Kayley

My boyfriend. He's paying for it. He'll kill me if I don't go through with it.

Paige

You've got to call the police about this abuse. You can't let him continue to hurt you.

Kayley

I'm breaking up with him after this! I plan to contact the police. I promise. But I need the operation.

Paige

Is the pregnancy termination your own choice?

Kayley

Yes! There's no other way. I can't even support myself, much less a baby. Besides, he'll kill me. He really will!

Paige

Dr. Brown's a good doctor. You'll be in good hands. But I need you to sign an extra release form and pay the extra cost. You do understand that the further along you are, the more likely you will have complications. [*Kayley nods.*] The extra release form will address those issues.

Kayley

Sure. I'll sign anything. [Kayley begins to sob, and Paige comforts her.] I was lying! Aaron didn't hurt me. He wouldn't hurt anyone. He's in jail and he needs drugs. I'm pregnant by one of the gang members. I don't even know who. I sleep with them in order to pay for the drugs. The gang really will kill me if I don't have this abortion. I have to sleep with them to supply Aaron with drugs. They're paying for me to be here, too!

Paige

Kayley, you can't live this way! You deserve to be free! Aaron needs to be in treatment. He does *not* need street drugs. The gang needs to be behind bars.

Kayley

I promise I'll go to the authorities as soon as I recover. Could I please sign the paper? I want to get this over with.

Paige

I'll quickly prepare the release form for you. You just lie down and try to relax. Do you need any magazines? [*Kayley shakes her head and Paige leaves the examination room.*]

<u>Act 1, Scene 4</u>

Outside the Baker Street Women's Clinic. Veronica is wide eyed as she walks toward the clinic. She looks at the group of sidewalk counselors assembled. They are carrying pro-life signs and praying. A uniformed police officer guards. Among the protesters is Mrs. Gillespie, Veronica's debate coordinator.

Mrs. Gillespie

Veronica, what are you doing here?

Police Officer

You are not to talk to the clients.

Veronica

That's okay. I'm not a patient and she's my teacher.

Mrs. Gillespie

What are you doing here?

Veronica

I was going to ask you the same thing. [*Looks down*] My dad works here on weekends. But he works at a hospital today. I didn't believe they performed abortions until I saw your signs.

Mrs. Gillespie

Christians for Life is in town for a convention. Does your dad live in this city?

Veronica

Yes. I'm spending vacation with him.

Mrs. Gillespie

How did you get to this clinic?

Veronica

I took a bus. [*Starts crying and her teacher puts her arms around her*]

[*Emergency sirens are heard. Circling lights shine on the sidewalk counselors. The police officer moves toward the sound of the sirens. Veronica and the others gaze in the same direction. After a few seconds, the police officer returns.*]

Police Officer

You are all going to have to clear the area. We've got an emergency situation.

Mrs. Gillespie

Oh no! Someone's going to need our prayers more than ever! [Veronica, Mrs. Gillespie and the other sidewalk counselors all leave the stage.]

<u>*Act 1, Scene 5*</u>

A holding room near a hospital ER. Priscilla Hogan, pale and dressed in a hospital gown lies on a bed. She is crying. Dr. Fleming walks in.

Hank

Priscilla, how are you feeling?

Priscilla

Rotten!

Hank

That's not surprising. Do you remember me pumping your stomach?

Priscilla

I remember someone doing it! It was stupid to overdose at the clinic.

Hank

I'm just glad Paige found you in time. [*Pauses*] I'm fond of you… You're the best nurse I know. A lot of people would have been very upset if you had… left us forever.

Priscilla

I've been depressed for weeks, Hank. I've tried counseling, but no one seems to understand what I go through at the job. No one! [*sobs*]

Hank

There are other nursing jobs. I could give you great references.

Priscilla

Even after this?

Hank

Yes, but first you need some hospitalization. You need to get stable and find a really good therapist. [*Pauses*] To be really honest, neither of us is cut out for performing abortions. [*Pauses*] I don't think anyone is.

Priscilla

For six months, I hoarded the Oxycontin and Dalmane. I got prescriptions from two different doctors for them. I felt powerful carrying them around like I could control my own destiny. Two weeks ago, I told Paige I was feeling queasy. She gave me the anti-nausea meds.

Hank

So you took the anti-nausea meds to keep down the other pills? [*Priscilla nods.*] Was there anything that happened today that led you to overdose?

Priscilla

Today, Paige broke her own policy and allowed a patient at 15 weeks gestation. Paige said that gang members would kill the girl if we didn't abort her. But we didn't have to do it. Paige could have called the police. I could have called the police. I watched that little baby on the sonogram screen, moving peacefully at first until… [*Cries hysterically*]

Hank

Oh Priscilla, you were just doing what you thought was right! We're both in a confusing business performing *legal services* to help women make the *right choices* about their *own bodies*. What a load of double-talk! What a crock of *double-think!*

Priscilla

I've known for some time that I was doing wrong. But I just didn't have enough energy to look for another job.

Hank

Your energy will return when your depression and anxiety alleviate. You've been through a lot for a long time.

[*Paige walks in.*]

Paige

Well, I'm glad to see you awake. You are the last person I would expect to overdose.

Hank

Paige, Priscilla needs her rest right now. I'm her doctor until she's taken upstairs.

[*Paige glares at Hank, but before she can say anything, an attendant comes in with a wheel chair.*]

Attendant

I've come o take Ms. Hogan to the fifth floor. Hello, Priscilla. [*Priscilla gets into the wheel chair.*]

Paige

[*Places Priscilla's purse in her lap*] If you give me your keys and tell me what to bring, I'll pack a bag for you.

Priscilla

Don't bother! [*The attendant pushes Priscilla through the door.*]

Paige

[*Angrily*] What's wrong with her? What's wrong with you? She's *my* nurse. I hired her. How dare you tell me not to talk to her!

Hank

[*Looks down*] We're both sick of the abortion business, Paige.

Paige

You said you were okay with it when I interviewed you!

Hank

That was seven months ago. I've reassembled the body parts of too many babies since then. I've heard too many women cry… after their procedures!

Paige

I told you it wouldn't be easy for a while. We all carry religious baggage.

Hank

It will never be easy for me. Or even acceptable any more. I can't live with myself right now. I truly understand how Priscilla became suicidal. Maybe I would be suicidal if I didn't have a daughter.

Paige

Okay, you're going to quit working at the clinic. But what about us.

Hank

I can't see you anymore if you stay in the business. You've got a cold side to you. You're not a monster, but you are cold!

Paige

I've been raped! I've told you about it. [*Hank nods.*] That was in medical school twenty years ago. Since the rape, I never let a man touch me. Not until you! [*Cries*]

Hank

[*Starts to hold Paige but stops*] You've experienced some true ugliness. You didn't deserve what happened to you. But can't you see? We're perpetuating the ugliness. I may not be as faith-filled as my ex-wife and daughter, but I believe that God made the babies that we kill. We have no right to shed innocent blood!

Paige

But what about the girls and women whose innocence is taken from them? Imagine raising a baby whose face is just like the man who battered you and spat on you! Not every woman who comes into our clinic has been raped, but some have. Some others have been forced into prostitution which is worse.

Hank

We'll never solve the problems by killing the innocent. We'll never agree on this.

Paige

[*Pauses. Page and Hank look at each other.*] When are you going to move your stuff out of the clinic? I've got to hire another physician soon.

Hank

Tonight. I'll leave the clinic keys in the flower pot near Friedan's window.

Paige

Stay with me one more night, Hank. Just one more night!

Hank
I can't. I've got to get home to Veronica.

Lights

<u>Act 1, Scene 6</u>

Lights up
Hank Fleming's residence. Hank walks in. His face is obviously tired and haggard. Veronica and Mrs. Gillespie stand up from the couch. Hank is surprised to see a strange woman. All present show uneasy expressions on their faces.

Veronica

Dad, this is Mrs. Gillespie. I told you about her. She's my debate coach.

Mrs. Gillespie

How do you do, Dr. Fleming.

Hank

Hello.

Mrs. Gillespie

I saw Veronica outside the Baker Street Women's Clinic today. I was behind the fence. I'm a sidewalk counselor.

Veronica

Dad, Friedan told me that you perform abortions.

Hank

I did but not anymore. I'm quitting. That's a promise. [*Hank and Veronica both cry, and Veronica throws her arms around her dad.*]

Mrs. Gillespie

We were at the clinic when an ambulance arrived. I pray the patient is still alive.

Hank

The ambulance wasn't for a patient. An employee got sick at the clinic. Since I've worked there, we haven't had any emergencies with patients. But it can happen at any time, and I won't be a part of it. I am truly finished!

Mrs. Gillespie

Thank the Holy Spirit!

Veronica

I love you so much, Dad!

Hank

And I love you… more than any other person on earth!

Veronica

Will you be honest with me, from now on?

Hank

I promise.

Veronica

Dad, you need to repent and ask Jesus into your heart.

Hank

I'll see about that. What I promise right now is that I'll read and study the Bible every day.

Mrs. Gillespie

That's a wonderful beginning!

[*Hank and Veronica hug again as the light fades.*]

THE END

Daughter of India

A Spiritual Biography of Camille Svensson

Cate Murray © 2020

Foreword

My late aunt, Camille Speer Svensson, spent many years as a Sanskrit scholar. She had studied under the eminent Sanskrit scholar, Judith Tyberg. By the early 1970s Camille and her husband became devotees of Sathya Sai Baba, an Indian guru. Camille translated the *Bhagavad Gita, the Atmagodha of Adi Sankara Charya, Five Upanishads,* and the *Brahma Sutras* for her spiritual leader.

Besides a scholar, my aunt was a loving, witty, generous person who considered me her own daughter.

When I wrote this biography, *Daughter of India,* I was a devotee of Sathya Sai Baba also. Today I am a Catholic Christian. A serious study of the Bible taught me that the Vedantic belief that every human is God, as Sai Baba taught, is the lie that the serpent told Eve. Although I no longer believe in most of Sai Baba's teachings, I decided to republish the biography of my aunt essentially as it was originally published in 2000. As I explain in the preface of this anthology, my paradigm or world view has changed over the years. By publishing writing revealing the tone of previous paradigms, I can honestly show where my belief and psyche were at different periods of my own life.

A human's relationship with God constitutes the most special bond in the universe. Even though Aunt Camille sought a false god, her effort shows she valued a quest away from a material world. My prayer is that Christ Jesus converted Aunt Camille, Uncle John, and my mother (who was also a devotee of SSB) as they lay unconscious before their physical deaths.

Camille's Roots and her Early Years

Camille's maternal grandmother, Louisa Jane Jackson, was born in 1848 in Alabama. She later changed her middle name to Texas in honor of her new state. Louisa's mother, Elizabeth Wahl, was of French and German extraction, and her father was of Scotch-Irish extraction. Possibly, Nathaniel Jackson was a first cousin of the famed Confederate general, Thomas (Stonewall) Jackson.

Louisa graduated from the Wetumpka Female Academy in Wetumpka, Alabama around 1863, then she married, became a physician, and lost her first husband by the time the Civil War ended. No doubt, the Latin and Greek that Miss Louisa studied at the girls' school aided her quick learning of medical terms. Her medical license aided her war torn homeland.

After the American Civil War, Camille's grandmother loaded a covered wagon with the few valuables left after Union troops vandalized their home and drove her parents and herself to Texas. According the family legend, one of Louisa's parents asked her, "Why Texas?" The young widow replied, "Because it's a new state!"

When Louisa changed her middle name, she acquired a new nickname, Lou T. When Lou T arrived in Texas, she discovered that it was less open to woman physicians than Alabama. However, her new homeland welcomed her skills as a midwife. Lou T would later pass midwifery skills to her daughter, Lelah, Camille's mother.

Camille's maternal grandfather, William Austin Cook, also moved from Alabama to Texas. William (Bill) served in the Confederate Army. After the war ended, Bill joined thousands of others in the migration westward. Farming was in his blood, so he bought a farm and also became a blacksmith in Bosque County in Central Texas. Bill was fluent in Spanish, so he became a notary public for Spanish speaking neighbors. At the time of his death, around 1886, he left two farms to 16 children and stepchildren, one being Camille's mother, Lelah.

Like Camille's maternal grandparents, her paternal grandparents also had Southern backgrounds. Amanda Thomas was born in Arkansas, and her roots extend back to Wales and Germany. Family legend states that Miss Amanda married beneath herself when she wed James Houston (Jim) Speer. One of Amanda's ancestors, probably a grandfather, had been a lord in Wales. As in many other Southern family legends, a drop of blue blood was overstated into a ton of inherited honor, courage, and entitlement. But no evidence shows that Amanda herself ever felt entitled. It is likely that she married Jim Speer for love, as opposed to marrying someone else because of his money or ancestry.

Jim Speer's mother, Sheba, is believed to have been a full-blood Cherokee Indian. His paternal grandfather, John Speer, emigrated from Scotland and settled in Arkansas where he became a Primitive Baptist preacher. John's son, Jacob, settled in Texas, became friendly with General Sam Houston, and helped rescue the general from the San Jacinto Battle field. Jacob's son, Jim, had the full name James Houston Speer after his father's friend.

Jim followed his father's footsteps into battle, serving in the Confederate Army during the Civil War.

Camille took pride in her Southern heritage for its pluck, graciousness, and hospitality. At the same time, she derided its slavery and racism. She always believed that African-Americans should be treated as human beings, equal to all others. Camille always adhered to Sai Baba's teaching: "There is one caste, the caste of humanity." But she enjoyed the tall tales, common to Southern families, and many good stories derive from a drop of so-called noble blood!

Because of a published collection of tales about early Bosque County history, some written chronicles exist about Camille's paternal grandfather, Jim Speer. *Ed Nichols Rode a Horse* by Ed Nichols and Ruby Nichols Cutbirth, a son in law and a granddaughter of Jim and Amanda Speer, features a story about Ed Nichols meeting the Speer family, including a little girl named Lynn (Camille's aunt), whom he later married. Nichols first worked for his future father in law as a young field hand, and later assisted him as a constable after Jim Speer was elected sheriff of Bosque County in 1884. Written under the general editorship of J. Frank Dobie, *Ed Nichols Rode a Horse*, published in 1943, is considered a classic by Texas rare book dealers.

While Jim Speer served as sheriff, his family lived in an apartment in the limestone jail. Camille's father, Hubert (Hub), recalled taking trays of meals from his mother's kitchen to the prisoners in their cells. While Texas was a frontier, rural sheriffs had the responsibility of tracking cattle, horse, and sheep thieves, as well as murderers. According to the stories in *Ed Nichols Rode a Horse*, Sheriff Jim Speer and Constable Ed Nichols worked well together and made Bosque County a safer place during those ominous years.

Unfortunately for the Speer family, Sheriff Jim Speer left his wife and children for another woman. Amanda Thomas Speer passed away soon after the abandonment, and at least five children were left homeless. Fortunately, Ed Nichols married Lynn Speer and Ed's mother provided a home for Ed, Lynn, and Lynn's siblings. The siblings included Hub who would later become Camille's father.

Hub Speer had little formal education because Bosque County had few schools, and school buses were nonexistent. Nevertheless, he displayed amazing ability with numbers, read books, and thought deeply. Hub took Socrates' advice and examined his life. He worked as a cowboy, a railroad worker, and finally as a financial supervisor of Scott and White Hospital in Temple, Texas. While working in Oklahoma as a cowboy, he met another cowboy named Will Rogers. The other boys in the outfit called Rogers "silly Willie," but Hub realized Rogers' genius and the two became lifetime friends. Camille had childhood memories of Will Rogers bouncing her on his knee.

Back home in Bosque County, Hub met, courted, and decided to marry a dark-haired beauty, Lelah Cook, daughter of Lou T and the late Bill Cook. Hub asked Miss Lelah to wait for him while he earned enough money to start a household. For about a year, Hub traveled with a railroad job, ate little more than beans, and saved his money. But when he went to collect the years-worth pay, the money was not available! A brother who closely resembled Hub had posed as him and collected the money for himself.

Hub and Lelah, nevertheless, married in 1900. Their financial resources were greatly diminished by Hub's dishonest brother. But the couple, who had both experienced poverty after losing a parent, were determined to make it financially. They were driven in that direction. Lelah ran boarding houses and engaged in the hard, constant work of cooking, cleaning, and sometimes babysitting for the boarders. Mrs. Speer continued running boarding houses even after her husband obtained prominence as a hospital financial supervisor.

The Great Depression wiped away much of the Speer savings, but Hub and Lelah were not daunted by financial obstacles; they began saving again. Mr. Speer especially believed in putting aside money for his children's education.

In 1901 Thomas King Speer was born to Hub and Lelah. He was a blonde-haired, academically-precocious, outgoing golden boy. Loura Camille followed on August 4, 1903. Her birthplace was Morgan, Texas.

Camille's birth year proved to be an historical landmark year. The Wright brothers demonstrated their thrilling, albeit short, airplane excursions in Kitty Hawk, North Carolina. Also in 1903, two Americans made history with the first successful cross-country automobile venture from New York City to San Francisco.

Camille's younger brother was born, around 1906, but he only lived about two years. It was common for families to lose children before the age of antibiotics and other medical advancements, but the loss of a child is always sad. Instead of admitting the hurt they felt, Camille's parents argued over what to put on the child's tombstone. Lelah called the boy "Michael" while Hub called him "Jackie." The tombstone at the Morgan, Texas cemetery bears the legend "Little Jackie," so evidently Hub won the argument.

On August 10, 1915 a baby girl was born to the Speer family. Despite entering this world two months premature, little Catherine Ellis Speer survived. Camille's younger sister was named for a family friend, Kathryn Ellis, a.k.a. Miss Kate. In the

1880s Miss Kate had courted the man who invented the popular drink, Dr. Pepper.

Camille was named for her paternal Aunt Loura and for a girlfriend of a maternal uncle. Years later, Camille's mother remarked, "I thought that girl (her brother's girlfriend) had the prettiest name I ever heard, so I decided to give it to Camille." Camille began her life with a beautiful name, but she felt little love from her mother. She was born at a time when her parents' marriage was unstable. Hub and Lelah separated around the time of Camille's birth. Only one in ten marriages ended in divorce at the time, and divorce was considered shameful. Hub and Lelah reunited and remained husband and wife until Hub's death in 1944.

Despite Lelah's lack of affection toward Camille, there was a wonderful, charitable side to her. Lelah was proud of Camille's beauty and made certain that her daughter was beautifully dressed and impeccably groomed. Camille's mother constantly fed and clothed the poor. She delivered babies to families who could not afford doctors, and she seldom charged for babysitting. Also, despite the unsavory (and potentially dangerous) nature of such tasks, Camille's mother often nursed the sick and washed and dressed deceased bodies.

Lelah generally loved children although her anger was often displayed on Camille. Remarkably, though, she would later become a loving mother-figure to Camille's only child.

A close bond took place between Camille and her older brother, Tommy. Camille and Tommy were both gifted children and stellar students, and they shared what the learned. Their mother favored Tommy over Camille, but the pair did not allow parental favoritism to shatter their bond.

Shortly after graduating from high school, Tommy became apprenticed to a lawyer. He had a magnetic personality, and he loved the cerebral work that law demanded. But the United States was soon involved in World War I. Newspaper editorials and speeches demanded that young men enlist, "make the world safe for democracy," and fight "the war to end all wars." Tommy either believed that his duty required him to fight, or he needed to escape a scandal, so he enlisted with the Canadians at 17. Too young to join the American military, he was soon killed in a French trench.

Years after her brother's death, Camille had an astral vision of her brother. Tommy appeared in a state of peace and happiness, and Camille finally felt at rest with her grief for both Tommy and little Jackie, the brother she had lost earlier.

After her son's untimely death, Lelah suffered from severe depression. She neglected Catherine who was only three at the time. Catherine started trekking across the railroad tracks to visit children whose parents allowed them to play in the mud. When Camille returned from school in the afternoon, she usually had to find her younger sister, bathe her, and feed her.

However, a divine hand alleviated Camille's worries two years later. One day, two nuns appeared on the Speers' doorstep. When Mrs. Speer saw the two medieval-dressed ladies, she felt fear. Camille's mother thought that nuns never came to Protestant homes except to announce a death in the family. One of the nuns said, "Your daughter, Catherine, has been attending our school every day. She is performing quite well, but we need some sort of payment in order to retain her."

Lelah was delighted. "Let me get my checkbook. I did not know where Catherine has been going, but she has been coming home so clean!"

Catherine, who was five by then, had gotten tired of playing in the mud. She wandered to a playground where dozens of children were swinging and jumping rope. When the bell rang, and the children went inside, Catherine followed them inside. Camille's sister found herself in a classroom with Sister Michael, an Irish nun. Since Catherine was a gifted child who had learned reading, writing, and simple arithmetic from her late brother, the five year old easily kept up with her seven year old classmates. Over the years, Catherine would tell stories about the no-nonsense Sister Michael.

In the early years, both Camille and Catherine suffered from stereotyping. They felt imprisoned by what people expected of them, rather than liberated to become who they really were. Others labeled Camille "the pretty one," and they labeled Catherine "the smart one." One day, the little sister asserted to her older sister, "I'm the smart one!" Camille replied, "It is easier to prove my beauty than your intellectual aptitude!" Despite the early stereotyping, both sisters grew up attractive, scholarly, and close.

Camille dazzled others with her deep blue eyes, her clear complexion, and her facial bones. She admitted, in her later years, that her extraordinary physical beauty provided an uncomfortable learning experience for her. "I would enter a restaurant, and people would put down their forks and knives and stare at me. Like others, Camille wanted to be treated like a person, not an object.

Her beauty made her popular with boys, but Camille did not want excess attention from them. She later admitted her puzzlement at the amount of candy and flowers she received. Tommy had told her to never let a boy kiss her, and she followed her brother's advice until her wedding day.

Camille felt propelled by her mother into her first marriage. Lelah was impressed by the young mechanic's presents of candy and his polite manners. Camille had finished high school, and wanted to attend college. Nevertheless, she took her mother's advice and got married.

The young husband had little knowledge of love or commitment. Camille tried to make the union work, but she found herself facing a path of obstacles. Divorce had become a less-taboo subject than it was when Camille's parents struggled with their marriage a generation earlier, but it was still a shocking topic. After being emotionally abused, the strong young woman was able to escape from her unhealthy bond by the means of a silly argument between her mother and her husband.

Lelah had cooked a steak for her son-in-law's lunch. He complained that the steak was tough, but Mrs. Speer kept insisting, "It is not tough!" After the foolish argument, Lelah decided that she did not like her son-in-law after all. She told Camille that any time she wished a release from her marriage, she would back her 100%. Camille was thankful for the encouragement and the means for an education. As she later explained, "Mama threw me into that unfortunate union, but she was like a *deus ex machina* to get me out!"

By the time of the divorce, Camille had a young son. For the child's sake, she and the baby moved into Mr. and Mrs. Speer's house. Lelah took care of little Hub, and Camille began attending

Mary-Hardin Baylor College in Belton, Texas. For a few years, she could be with her beloved son while pursuing her own education.

Camille earned an education degree in 1925, but she was well-versed in the liberal arts. She also received training in languages and journalism. Besides English, she learned to speak Spanish passably well, and delighted herself with classical Greek. Later in life, she studied Sanskrit under Judith Tyberg. She finally became a Sanskrit scholar herself.

Besides teaching in various schools, Camille read voraciously, traveled, and enjoyed playing bridge. She won a bridge prize of a trip to Deauville, France. In Deauville, she won another bridge tournament. While in Mexico with friends, Camille played an American tourist in a Mexican film.

Despite her interesting family tree and her fascinating life, the spiritual woman would seldom talk about the worldly aspects of her life. She once said, "What I did yesterday, I vomit today." She took Sathya Sai Baba's advice: "The past is past; do not waste time looking back on the road you have traversed" (*Sathya Sai Speaks* Vol. X, p. 53).

People Like You Are Needed

At birth Camille possessed a certain amount of clairvoyance and clair audience, but she became extremely clair audient after she contracted a ghastly illness and nearly died. In 1935, after swimming in the San Antonio River, she became gravely ill with Typhoid Fever. Without her knowledge, sewage had been dumped into the river. Oddly, the seemingly careless action of city workers helped provide Camille with a transforming experience.

Friends took Camille to a San Antonio hospital. She was in critical medical condition. In her later years, she recounted her "death" experience, for she truly believed she had died:

I, without a physical body, with a very expanded, blissful, unattached consciousness was standing, yet with no sense of actually standing, but "being" in the corner of the hospital room. I knew that my body was lying on the hospital bed, packed in ice with a temperature of 108—I also "saw" the chart that was placed at the foot of the bed. The temperature had reached that altitude eight other times, but had been arrested and lowered. I seemed to know everything, but was not reacting in any emotional way. The scene arrived more vivid than [any] ordinary scene looked with me with the physical eyes—the colors were very beautiful. I noticed that the young intern was chewing gum and had Oriental features. I heard him say to the nurse, my mother, and a lady friend, "She is totally collapsed." The nurse then pulled the pillow out from under my head—reading thoughts was as easy as hearing words, so I knew she wanted me to die with my body straight.

*I was suddenly out of the hospital room leaving the earth
very fast. I seemed to be traveling in a vacuum tube with invisible
sides. I looked down on the earth—saw it—felt completely
unattached. There was no joy, no sorrow in leaving it—just pure
peaceful bliss. I was not missing having a body at all, but seemed
to be covered with beautiful, glowing colors as though through a
garment. A very strong and forceful light appeared on one side of
me. Very strong and forceful: it arrested my upward flight—a
clear voice said,* **"People like you are needed on earth."** *I was
then forced down even more rapidly than I had been forced up. I
was very quickly back in the hospital room I had left and put back
into my body—I felt a sharp pain which seemed to be in every cell
of my body—pain impossible to endure. I lost consciousness, and
did not gain normal consciousness for several weeks. I weighed
50 pounds. My normal weight was 115. My recovery was rapid
and excellent with no permanent defect from the illness other than
premature white hair.*

After regaining consciousness, Camille visited with her son.
She asked him what he was studying in school, and he began
talking about the Nile River. Camille commented, "Yes, that great
river in Africa." When Hub insisted that the Nile River was not in
Africa, Camille, temporarily, thought that her memory had been
affected. But she soon realized that it her young son who was
mistaken, not she.

While Camille recovered from her illness, she began
changing her lifestyle. No longer did she eat rare steaks and drink
champagne cocktails. She became a vegetarian and a teetotaler.
She lost interest in novels, theater shows, and movies with no
spiritual meaning. The thirty-two year old woman gave up bridge

tournaments and even bridge games. When others asked her about the film that she had been in, she changed the conversation. For a time, before her white hair grew in, the once-glamorous lady was bald. Even the alteration of her appearance did not daunt her. Camille believed her new life had meaning.

While Camille's body healed from its ordeal, her mind, her intuition, and her gifts of clairvoyance and clair audience became clearer and keener.

In a talk Camille gave in her later years, she explained to others that having such gifts of sight and hearing is not always pleasant. "Sometimes I would see and hear what I did not wish to." When she perceived things that would interest or benefit others, Camille realized that she must exercise care about giving readings. She believed that readings must be given for spiritual purposes only, and if she took money for readings, she would lose the gifts.

Camille began having astral visions of the Chinese Goddess of Mercy, Quan Yin. She would often tell others how beautiful, kind and healing Quan Yin was to her. Later, when Camille was in her 60's and 70's, she would wear a coral, pearl, and diamond pin of the goddess. Her bedroom in her San Pedro home contained several figurines of the Chinese goddess.

After her clairvoyant visions intensified, Camille's intuition led her to study Theosophy. Theosophy combines philosophy, religions (especially Eastern religions), and science in order to "collect and diffuse a knowledge of the laws which govern the universe" (Blavatsky). For over 30 years, Camille lectured and taught classes for the Theosophical Society.

In the late 1960s Camille began work on a biography of Madame Helena Petrovna Blavatsky, a co-founder of Theosophy.

She traveled to England to research her book, but ran into disagreements with Quest Publications. Camille explained, "I discovered Blavatsky was not a spiritual as I had believed her to be."

Camille's sister, Catherine, tried to persuade her to find another publisher, but the older sister decided to cancel the project altogether.

While lecturing for the Theosophical Society on nights and weekends, Camille taught elementary school on weekdays. She had begun teaching in Texas, but she later taught in the Los Angeles Independent School System for 30 years. Camille's first classroom experience in an inner city school demanded much strength. Many of the young children came from homes where morality and human values were not taught. But soon Camille's guidance changed the children's thinking and calmed them down, so they could respect each other and learn.

The only time she would allow vulgar words in the classroom was when a new child registered in the middle of a term. Camille was known as Mrs. Leigh then, and as part of the new student's orientation, a class leader would say, "Mrs. Leigh don't want to hear that. She don't want to hear !@*% or @!)^! Youngsters realized that they could not even whisper inappropriate language because one of Camille's gifts was clair audience.

After Mrs. Leigh demonstrated success with inner-city children, she was placed with children who were partially visually handicapped. Her love for all children, her eagerness to learn new ways to help her students overcome handicaps, and her belief that a teacher must instill values in the classroom engendered successful teaching. Many of the children bonded with Camille, and some even cried when summer vacation rolled around.

Camille provided several children with the only stable environment they had known.

Camille believed that children, as well as adults, should read stories that teach values in order to build character. From time immemorial till just a few generations ago, stories taught a moral code such as the Christian one: "Do unto others as you would have them do unto you." She worked with youngsters that daily encountered temptations to hit others, steal, or break windows because they felt anger or coveted the possessions of neighbors. Camille knew that if children acted on their present temptations, they could act on more serious desires later. She knew that both parents and teachers needed to point youth in the right direction.

The Avatar

The near-death experience changed Camille's life immensely, but meeting a man, whom she believed to be a divine avatar or God in the flesh, changed her profoundly. She perceived that Sathya Sai Baba would point her in the direction of her own divine mission.

Her fourth husband, John Svensson, joined her in her spiritual journey. After three failed marriages, she had believed that she would never again enter the matrimonial state. However, in the 1940s, a psychic friend told her that in the last 30 years of her life she would be married, living in a beautiful house by the ocean, and she would be happy. All these predictions generally became true. In 1966 Camille married Captain John Osborne Svensson, moved to his home in San Pedro, worked out their personality differences, and became content with each other.

John was born in Sweden in 1910. His father was often gone on long fishing voyages, so John often helped his mother with the six younger children. When he was only 15, he left home and became a sailor on a merchant marine ship. Before maritime unions, captains could abuse young sailors without mercy. Harsh treatment either turned a boy into a man, or it broke his spirit. John turned his hardship into a learning experience and became a captain while he was still in his twenties.

Not only did John learn nautical terms and the maritime skills, he also taught himself English during his off-duty hours. English speaking seamen can communicate with Americans, Canadians, Australians, Britons, Indians, and many others. In 1938 the young captain became an American citizen. By then,

John had married his first wife and fathered a baby daughter. The couple later had a son.

World War II proved a demanding time for merchant seamen. John was in the line of danger longer than most other Americans that served in the armed services. The Allied Forces needed great quantities of fuel to run the planes, tanks, and jeeps. Since Europe did not produce its own oil, ships carrying oil were vital to the war effort. From 1948 until 1945, John captained explosive oil tankers in waters teeming with hidden Nazi submarines. He witnessed a tanker in close proximity to his explode. Miraculously, John's tanker was not struck.

Two elderly British ladies introduced John to Theosophy aboard a passenger ship he was navigating. The women sensed John's anguish at his separation from his family. When he expressed his wish that life held more than frustrations and worldly success, the women enthusiastically replied, "It certainly does!"

More than a decade after joining a Theosophy group, he attended a session lectured by Camille. Around that time John retired after serving more than 30 years as a sea captain and became a maritime pilot for the Los Angeles Harbor of San Pedro. Unfortunately, throat cancer soon claimed John's wife. He later married Camille in 1966.

In the early 1970's, Camille and John entertained Theosophist Howard Murphet in their home. Mr. Murphet was also a Sathya Sai Baba devotee, and he introduced the Svenssons to his spiritual leader.

As a journalist Murphet had covered the Nuremberg trials, so he well knew that humans are capable of unspeakable cruelty. Worldwide, many people lost faith in God after learning about the

Nazi horrors. The question generally asked was, "How could a loving, merciful God allow six million innocent people to be enslaved, starved, beaten, tortured and executed?" Howard Murphet asked that question but did not lose faith in God.

The Australian jounalist believed that every hardship is earned by karmic debt. He also believed that no matter how horrific these punishments are, God never abandons his children.

As Camille and John's houseguest, Murphet told the Svenssons about Baba's many miracles. Camille and John were skeptical at first. In their studies of Theosophy, they believed that a true avatar exhibited several analytical points of identification. They further pointed out that many yogis had misused their powers by falsely posing as avatars. Obeying the false gods seriously harmed many devotees. Therefore, an alleged avatar must be approached cautiously.

At the time Mr. Murphet told Camille about Sai Baba, Camille was so prudent about not being mislead that she followed no gurus of any kind. Instead, she preferred to study and translate the Upanishads herself. "I had no gurus along the way," she explained in a talk given in the 1980's. But when her friend told her about Sai Baba's raising of the dead, healing the crippled, and creating jewelry seemingly from thin air, Camille's mind opened up. "If he [Sathya Sai Baba] can do all that, he probably is an avatar" she concluded.

The most important point of identification for an avatar, to Camille, was Divine Grace. As she explained in the 1980's talk, there are two kinds of Divine Grace that an avatar bestows upon human beings. One type of grace is given to a person because he or she has earned it karmically. Another type of grace is granted by the avatar to the human simply out of Divine Love.

Knowing that Camille possessed gifts of clairvoyance and clair audience, Mr. Murphet encouraged her to contact Sai Baba through these extrasensory gifts. She took her friend's advice and experienced what she termed "waves of love" from Sai Baba. She believed that Murphet's spiritual leader had sent her what her heart had always longed for—the inner God. She immediately began telling her sister and her circle of friends about her wondrous discovery.

No matter how busy Camille was with her teaching or her lecturing, she always found time for others. She once remarked, "When I travel, I go to see people. I do not sightsee. I don't seek entertainment." One reason Camille had time for others was because she never watched television. She and John kept a TV in order to watch videos of Sai Baba, but they never filled their lives with the latest disaster on the news shows or the latest fads on the sitcom shows. Camille once said, "I find life itself fascinating. I don't have to seek artificial life from a television set."

Camille spent her leisure time writing to others, especially to her sister, Catherine, and her new Sai friends. The distant relationship between Camille and Catherine became close after the older sister introduced her younger sister to Sathya Sai Baba. When Camille first became a devotee, and she wrote to Catherine about her avatar, Catherine insisted, "He [Sai Baba] is just another Hindu. I'm a Buddhist."

When Catherine visited Camille and John in late 1972, their conversations centered on Sai Baba. Catherine listened but expressed disvomfort over Baba's alledged manifestation of jewelry. She felt that an avatar had greater and more important things to do. Camille wanted her sister to hear the stories of other devotees, so they and several others traveled to Tecate, Mexico to visit Indra Devi, the famous yoga instructor and Sai Baba devotee.

Catherine appreciated Indra Devi's graciousness, but she did not convert immediately after meeting her. But when Camille's younger sister met Mr. and Mrs. Walter Cowan, the conversion was instantaneous. Mr. Cowan believed he had died and was raised from the dead by Sai Baba.

"I met Lazarus!" Catherine declared after meeting Mr. Cowan. "And here is the man that lifted Lazarus!" Camille's sister would say after showing the picture of Sai Baba that Mr. and Mrs. Cowan had given her.

The two sisters embarked on their first trip to India to meet Sai Baba in 1974. They traveled with several other devotees and aspirants. The spiritual leader allegedly materialized pendants for Camille and Catherine. Pictures of Baba decorated the pendants. After the 1974 pilgrimage, Camille returned home to John and related her experiences. He also became a devotee.

In October 1981 Camille's faith was tested when she tragically lost her sister Catherine to organ failure following heart surgery. The rheumatic fever that the younger Speer sister had suffered at five years old weakened her heart for life. In 1952 Catherine had traveled to Philadelphia to undergo her first open heart surgery. It was successful, but her second surgery was not, despite Catherine's choice of a Sai Baba devotee as a surgeon.

Camille admired her younger sister's courage. Catherine had been a survivor throughout her 66 years. She obtained a BA in French, an MA in philosophy, and an instructor position at the University of Texas. She later married, had her first daughter, helped her husband with his real estate business, and became a pillar in the Lake Whitney community. Catherine's second daughter was born 15 months after her first open heart surgery.

Following Baba's instructions, Camille and John's home became the Sathya Sai Baba Center of San Pedro. The Svenssons provided worship services, study, and bhajan (hymn) singing for devotees and aspirants. For a number of years, leaders of other centers met at Camille and John's home for the monthly district meetings.

The Svenssons made several pilgrimages to Sai Baba in the 1970's and 1980's. According to their spiritual leader, Camille had been a pundit in a previous life. The word **pundit** has attained a secular meaning recently in American English. Yet, the word derives from the Sanskrit word *panditah* meaning "a learned person" or "an authority" (*American Heritage Concise Dictionary,* 670). In ancient times, "a learned person" studied sacred scriptures and taught the scriptural knowledge and wisdom to others.

Sai Baba not only deemed Camille "a pundit," he also gave her a title, "Daughter of India," hinting that she had lived more than one previous life in India.

Camille's spiritual leader encouraged her to continue translating sacred literature and to publish her translations. She followed his council, and in 1985 the Sathya Sai Baba Society published Camille's translation of the *Bhagavad Gita,* with exegeses from the writings of Bhagavan Sri Sathya Sai Baba. The Sathya Sai Baba Society issued a second printing in 1992.

In Indian religious writings, the *Bhagavad Gita* is an epic within the longer epit, *The Mahabharata. The Mahabharata* expounds upon the causes, effects, and aftermath of a great war between noble relatives, the five sons of Pandu and their cousins, the hundred sons of Dhritarashtra. Although *The Mahabharata* and the *Bhagavad Gita* fall outside the canon known as the *Upanishads,* Sai Baba stated that the *Bhagavad Gita* is "the essence of the *Upanishads."*

The Upanishads consists of various groups of poetic and prose philosophical treatises contributing to the theological foundation of ancient Hinduism. The treatises elaborate on the *Vedas,* the oldest Hindu texts. According to Hindus, *The Upanishads* and the *Vedas* address and clarify the Vedantic principle that all existence (including humankind) is one and the same with the omniscient, omnipresent, and benevolent God.

Camille believed Sai Baba's claim that he was an incarnation of the avatar Krishna, the charioteer and guide of the hero, Arjuna, in *The Bhavagad Gita.*

While translating the *Gita*, Camille dedicated all her activities to the man who she believed was the Lord of the Universe. As a pundit and a Daughter of India, she discovered that she could best serve God by translating Sanskrit into her native tongue. Following the translation of *The Bhagavad Gita,* Camille translated the *Atmabodha,* the *Yoga-Sutras of Patanjali,* and the *Brahma Sutras*.

According to Sai Baba, John also had roots in India. In a previous lifetime, John had been a devotee of Shirdi Sai Baba, allegedly a previous incarnation of Sathya Sai Baba. Baba gave John a ring, and he claimed the ring had belonged to Shirdi Sai Baba. The ring was set in silver, and the Om symbol was etched in the blue stone setting.

Dr. Samuel Sandweiss, who was a San Diego psychiatrist, describes the event of John receiving the ring in his book, *Spirit and the Mind.* Sandweiss cites Baba as saying:

Blue is the color of the infinite—that which cannot be measured, that which is unfathomable...the sky is blue and the ocean is blue. Blue is a cool color. It is peaceful. Look around, all the doctors in the room are wearing blue—it comforts and soothes (190).

Shortly after receiving the gift, the setting fell out. On the next trip to India, John showed the blue stone and the silver. "You are too hard on rings!" the spiritual leader told him.

Camille's last trip to India would also be disappointing. She began exhibiting early signs of dementia. Her memory started failing, and she would ask others, including members of Catherine's family, "Did you know Catherine?"

For several years, John lovingly cared for Camille after she was unable to care for herself. Camille's physician determined that she was not afflicted with Alzheimer's disease; rather, Camille had apparently been suffering from a series of small strokes. After she broke her hip, John placed Camille in a local nursing facility. He continued caring for her by visiting her daily, reading to her, and praying over her.

Camille's other family members and friends also spent loving hours with her during the last years. Although she could not speak toward the end, she would look into faces and indicate if she recognized someone.

Succumbing to pneumonia, Camille passed away on July 19, 1998. Her body was cremated, and John deposited her ashes in the Pacific Ocean two miles south of the Los Angeles Harbor Lighthouse. Later, on August 29, John and Camille's friends held a memorial service for her at the Sathya Sai Baba Book Center in

Tustin, California. The service included devotional singing and eulogies by John and close friends. The pamphlet given at her memorial service also paid tribute to Camille Speer Svensson's life:

Camille Svensson was a devotee of Sathya Sai Baba for many years. She worked tirelessly to help people know about Swami's teachings. Camille was very successful in that endeavor because she herself practiced Swami's teachings. She was an intellectual giant and a great bhakta. She was a mother to many of us, a teacher, a friend to all, and an inspiratiion to everyone.

Sources

American Heritage Concise Dictionary, 3rd ed.
Houghton Mifflin, 1994.

Blavatsky, Helena P. *The Secret Doctrine.*
Theosophical U P, 1888.

Sandweiss, Samuel H. *Spirit and the Mind.* Birth
Day Publications, 1986.

Sathya Sai Speaks. Sathya Sai Society. n.d.

Svensson, Camille (trans.). *Bhagavad Gita or The
Divine Song with Comments Taken from the
Writings of Bhagavan Sri Sathya Sai Baba.*
Sathya Sai Society, 1985.

Poetry

1953

Seven years after Nuremberg,

In the summer of the Rosenbergs,

Forceps guided me into the world

Of musical teddy bears and Borax.

Armed with two saints' names,

Rather than a Biblical first

With a Southern middle,

I was announced on the front page.

Babies were submerging the heroes.

We were bottle-fed and weighed daily.

I picture my pink-ruffled nursery

Not unlike the sunny nursery-dorms

In Bavaria a decade before.

America had become the greatest museum.

She wore a wedding ring of Tungsten Steel.

Everyone else, before Sputnik, was Brand X.

Headlines about Indochina were often sandwiched

Between babies and beauty queens.

The black and white of Ike
And Speedy Alkaseltzer filled home after home.
Solutions seemed as easy
As Reddy Kilo-Watt.

My family bought a new T.V.
The year I came.
It lasted seven years.

Birthmother

Did she daydream about being married to my father?
Lying beside him, listening to him breathe
like the tide at night?
Or was he someone almost faceless to her,
a body she coupled with after too many beers?

Did I move inside her like a stretching ballerina,
or did I wiggle like a maggot
she couldn't get rid of?

Did she tell her mother when she discovered me,
or did she try to hide me under tent dresses?

I've heard strange stories about girls
who told themselves their tummies
were full of nothing but ice cream;
like any balloon, they would flatten again.
The girls weren't bothered by the curse every month,
so they forgot about it,
just as they tried to forget about the boys
who quit calling them.

Did the other girls in her gym class
guess me before she did,
or did she fake the curse
to buy some quiet time with me?

I can only picture her
as the girl I read about in my files –
short red hair, shy, interested in water colors and fashion design.
Does she think of me as the little bundle with the elfin face,
or does she search for mirrors
in every young woman's eyes?

When I celebrate my life every April 26,
does she feel a death without a funeral?

Sometimes I want to know;
sometimes I want to keep the book closed.

BLOOD KIN IN WAR

Texas War for Independence:
Great-great Grandpa Speer
Rescued Sam Houston from the
San Jacinto field.

Civil War:
Youngster foot soldiers,
Gray shirts like Athena's eyes,
Fed hardtack and squirrel.

One Union private,
Fled cruel uncle and drafted,
Friends' faces ripped; cold.

WWI:
Escaping scandal,
Tom joined the Canadians,
Booby trapped in trench.

Grandpa Murray's crop
failure; took government job
Guarding armaments.

WWII:
Hub flew Venturas,
Dodged German anti-aircraft;
Polio killed him.

Vedantic Puzzle

The part is nothing –
a fragment, figment, a virus.
The part becomes the Whole.
Forget about the part, the maya.
Focus on the Whole: the Real.

But my part was very real:
It could feel
and reason
and move
and dance
and LOVE.

It had a will
to be very still
and listen to the One, True God.

The Memoirs of Miss Rose Shaw

Few men's faces I can think of.
Sometimes I recall a red and black hotel room.
The boom towns were like brothers –
Whiskey smells with a pulled shade.

Once I lived a week in Sweetwater –
A gentleman courted me in grand style.
He sent me roses and poems each morning
And took me to dinner at night.

One Sunday morning, I found no flowers,
No poems, just silent words.
A girl like m shouldn't have been dreamin'
Trimmed in Shakespeare-words and fancy gloves.

I'm told I'm bright for ninety-three,
I still have vinegar and fire.
Young magazine girls consider me an almanac,
I'm just Rose and nothin' else.

Marilyn and Sylvia

> *"Last night, in a dream, Marilyn Monroe*
> *appeared to me as a fairy godmother.*
> *She gave me an excellent manicure,*
> *and we talked about men."*
> *Sylvia Plath – Journal, 1959*

Aphrodite and Erudite,
coin-twins cast in different caste systems.
One inside they feel unwanted
as a box of kittens.

They bleach their hair baby-blonde,
paint their lips with red smiles,
and go out in search of Daddy.
Several scrapbooks later, one finds a President
with Rhett Butler rhetoric;
the other charms an anthropologist
with a voice like Thor.

But when the curtain closes, they're alone.
Marilyn with her telephone, pills and secret diary;
Sylvia with her poison pen, brandy and Beethoven.

The goddesses called from the labyrinth,
but the echoes came too late.

A Depressed Woman's Psyche

A depressed woman's psyche
is like a john that won't flush.
All the abortions and engagement rings,
all the rejection letters and intercepted notes
rise to the top for everyone to see.

The neighbors know.
She tries to smile as she asks to borrow
a plunger and 7 valium.
They offer her cake and champagne,
and invite her to church.
After she leaves, they whisper
about her unwashed hair
and about the smell coming from her house.
Other neighbors talk on the phone.
They discuss which casseroles to bring to her wake.
When they think she is asleep,
they come and plant more weeds in her garden.

Fetal eyed, the depressed woman sees
all the needles and daggers pointed at her.
Panting dogs laugh at her.
In the dark, her head feels
the endless noise of bad radios.

Deconstruction

The child took apart
the antique clock
and invented
his own strange toy –
bling, blang, klang, crash.

Under the Bell Jar

The Lady of the Lake
lies under the bell jar.
Excalibur hides somewhere under her folds
like a crippled dwarf.

Lifting the bell jar
is not as easy
as extracting a firm Excalibur
from an ancient stone.
Riddles and potions work like leeches
on the children of Descartes.
Magic names cannot penetrate the diaphragm.
Fossilized eggs sit in a canopic jar.

41 Fitzroy Road

Candlemas with no quickening;
white morning with no red dawn.
The Norns spin their last curse.

I must leave before the children awake;
before the tulips arrive.
The brandy and the Beethoven feel more like bennies;
I command the sleep they refused.

Cat-footed, I place the milk and the bread
at the children' nightable.
They are faceless now.
I close the door, cut the cords.
I seal the cracks.

Yeats' spirit has vanished from this flat.
So has mine.
As Anne says, "Suicide is the opposite of a poem."

I open the door and turn the button of my fate.
I create a Dachau
to escape all Dachaus.

Hope

I vision myself
rescuing my heart chakra
from its canopic jar –
I massage and breathe into it
like a midwife
trying to save an abandoned infant.
I call upon the God-force
that first warmed the arctic night –
The wise, old grandmother who concocted
the recipe for protoplasm.

The Speech of Uta Renner
*(An elderly woman receives a medical award for her father who
was killed by a Germantown mob in 1917.)*

In this country of monuments,
Real heroes often die unknown.
They are devoted to duties, not performances,
And quietly mend what others have torn.

Since my father's death,
It appears we have set a goal
To cure death itself.
Yet, despite antibiotics,
Immunizations, and microscopic surgery,
Man builds clever warheads,
And settles feuds with tanks.

We have become too dependent on leaders
Elected on single issues.
But if we depend on others,
We are controlled by others,
And we are back to the time
Of kings and emperors.

In the words of Hermann Hesse:
"Only within yourself exists
That reality for which you long."
I say, "Separate meditation
Is where we belong."

Across the Street
From the Methodist Church

Once we lived across the street
From a big, Methodist church.
It was white and had
Blue and butterfly windows.

On Sunday mornings, I'd wake,
Hearing their songs
As Mother carried me
To the house after Mass.

Later, I'd join
The Children on the lawn,
Trading my holy pictures for theirs –
Blessed Mary and the saints
For Jesus and Moses.
Girls would take turns
Wearing my rosary around their necks.

I thought the Methodist's Jesus
Had never been on a cross.
I felt Him around –
In the sky, in the trees,
And under the water.

First Communion Day

Scraping mud from my shoes,
And brushing a caterpillar from my sock,
I waited in line
With the other brides and grooms.

Shifting the big candle to my other hand,
I breathed in the holy smell.
Bells frightened the birds
From the cross,
And we began marching to our front row pews.

It was dark in the confessional yesterday.
Father Moore sounded like the Wizard of Oz.
I cried, trying to remember all my sins,
Thinking of the dotted picture
Of the unclean soul.

I prayed until Mass was over.
I was glad I remembered to kneel.
My stomach felt empty but my heart was filled.
Above, the sycamore leaves clapped.

Mother's Books

Daddy used to laugh and say sometimes the house would
split open and out would come books, books, books.
At least once a year a carpenter would come and build
more shelves – in the living room, the kitchen, the garage.
My sister said it was embarrassing to let guests
use the bathroom, it was so full of paperbacks.
Mother was every pulp writer's dream
of a great American citizen – she bought.
    When Daddy dragged in from a day of selling real estate,
Mother fortified him with a highball while she
dramatized the lines of Max Brand or Zane Grey.
Other nights, he watched Gunsmoke or Have Gun, Will Travel
while she read Agatha Christie or Mickey Spillane.
At least twice Mother wrote a letter to Taylor Caldwell
asking her to write more books,
until we went to Europe and she discovered Dennis Wheatley,
a British writer, a Tory, of course,
who shared her fascination of the psychics,
and wrote thrillers and historical novels
based on facts from the
waste paper baskets of non-fiction editors.
"I think he's married to Joan Grant!"
she theorized excitedly.
    Books cured everything, Mother thought.
We'd all get books, not chicken soup, for the flu.
Uncle Ralph got Ayn Rand when he had eye surgery.
Somehow Mother convinced the Lion's Club that
a county bookmobile would take care of
the problem of juvenile delinquency.
    I finally got up the nerve to check out an ancient copy
of Dear Abby Talks to Teenagers About Sex.
Mother found it and gave me three of her James Bond's.

"He fights the Communists," she explained.

Mrs. Bonham

In Mrs. Bonham's drafty living room,
Crocheted doilies covered the old furniture,
And a dusty Last Supper
Hung from the wall.
I'd stand, shivering in my petticoat,
Terrified she'd forget I wasn't a pin cushion.
Mrs. Bonham would whisper
To my grandmother while my nose would wrinkle
From the mingling smells
Of gas from the heater and onions from the kitchen.

Sometimes I'd catch odd words,
"Railroad baby", "bootleg moonshine", "barn horse".
Other times, Grandma would raise her hand
To Mrs. Bonham's mouth,
Put on a smile for me, and remark
What a pretty dress I'd soon have,
Or ask Mrs. Bonham about this year's petunias.

I later learned Mrs. Bonham kept nine-month
Calendars as proof, often forgetting
To regard the extra days
Of longer months.
She'd bring the calendars to prayer-meetings,
Along with the Bible and pies.

No one keeps much of a calendar for Mrs. Bonham
Now that she's gone.
I wonder what she'd think being buried
Near a car thief, two drunks, and a Catholic.
Only once have the Eastern Stars

Adorned her grave with flowers.
The epitaph reads, "Gone, but not forgotten."

Christmas Fruitcake

On the Monday after Kennedy died,
Mother taught me how to make Christmas fruitcake.
　We faced each other in the kitchen-den
Mother and Daughter aprons
photos of cows　antique rifles hung on duck heads
　"Tell me what we've done so far.
Start with the sugar and butter."
Mother quizzed me on cakes
Like she quizzed me on saints or the Texas Senate.
　"Add some more fruit and nuts," she said.
I cut cherries and dates
with the same scissors I snatched that night
to cut discarded news for my secret scrapbook.
　Over by the T.V., with the masking tape "X"
Mother grabbed the phone.
"Oh yes. Yes, we have a much better chance
of winning next year!
　I checked the chopped nuts for shells,
then poured them into the bowl of red and green,
thinking about the sticker I tore from the bumper,
"Kennedy for King
Goldwater for President."
　Mother changed ears.
"That damned Irish priest!
An hour and a half for a sermon…"
　"How long can this cake last?"
I finally thought of something to say.
"Longer than the last President!" She laughed
as she placed the pan in the oven.
"After you finish the dishes,
I'll show you how to make marzipan icing…"

GIRL

Too old to cry
too unimportant to talk
too restless to sit
too strong to quit

Adolescence

Once upon a person's age,
Lasting only a few centuries of years,
The senses are both haunted and enchanted,
Altering mirrors and dividing kingdoms.
Sometimes last spring's prince does not grow enough
To become the autumn knight.
He watches while his former pages,
Adorned in helmets and armor-pads,
Crown the homecoming queen, a former swine,
This new queen, only a few hours prior,
Wept tears of both humiliation and delight
Upon finding that last season's bra
Fit like Cinderella's slipper
On her stepsister's foot, then wept more tears
Of delight while gazing at her old gown,
Swallowing her aw if she were Goldilocks
In Papa Bear's chair. After repainting her eyes and smile,
She rides off with a former dwarf
In a borrowed Porsche-pumpkin.

Of course, there are those who simply never quite
Make it to royalty, dreams or no dreams.
If a dwarf is a joiner, he might organize his own group
In pursuit of a Snow White, perhaps forgetting
That she gets the prince in the end,
Or perhaps the boy becomes a Rumpelstiltskin,
Cleverly showing the maiden how to catch her prince,
Then demanding, as payment, that she do his English project.

As for girls, well, a few may turn from swine to witches,

Purging themselves after feasting on the candy
And gingerbread house. But more often than not,
There is merely the matter of a damsel's
Slightly irregular nose haunting her
Like a pea under a mattress. She may stay home
On Saturday nights until she meets the lad
With a chin so deformed it won't grow a beard.

We cannot promise happily ever after,
Though most episodes finally do end,
Some people return by crashing, others by growing,
But few sail through a peaceful wind.

For Ginny

Small graduating classes
Always have someone who's legendary –
The girl who's sent no Valentines
But a bottle of wine
From the football team;
The girl who arrives without a date
To the prom, but dances every dance.
This girl would sit alone at lunch,
Reading Dickinson or Gibran,
Her soft hair flowing past
Her cheeks and shoulders.
     She made no sound
When the class president
Was given valedictorian;
Most beautiful was a cheerleader
Who chewed bubblegum
And wore turquoise eye-shadow.

Buried in the back of the yearbook,
She receives no credit
For the teams and the clubs
She could not join.
     It seems, now, she was always
Like the paintings in which
She's famous –
Skies with doors
And flowers inside of a seed.

For My Mother
August 10, 1915 – October 7, 1981

As I walk away from your waxy face and arms
Hitched to machine cords,
From that room lewd with anesthesia,
I can almost hear you arguing with God.
I take my place in the boxlike waiting room
With the stone faces of the rest of my family.

Sitting on a cold, hard chair
Below a buzzing clock, my throat tightens
With each swallow of wine.
I race through the years we shared
And the moments we tore each other apart.
You once told me about the cardiologist
Who wanted you to get rid of me in Havana.
You became a stepmother sometimes
When you tied me to the kitchen table
With McGuffey's primers.
I made pictures from the words
And words from the pictures.
You told me I could not marry
Without a Ph.D.
You later told me Daddy burned
Your dissertation on Henri Bergson
Thinking it was killing you.

Seldom praying to the same saints
Or supporting the same candidates,
We both grew, separately, our firm roots
Occasionally touching.

Hearing footsteps coming closer,
I want to sit under a tree alone.
Part of me wants to bring you back
So we can set each other free.
But inside I know you understand.
Go in peace, Mother.

The Cave Temple

Only God could have carved the bliss
in Buddha's face.
He sits, 30 feet above me, in the dark coolness of a
petrified forest.

For a thousand years he has meditated here.
For a thousand years he has filled this air
with eternal incense.

In his hands he weaves a seed with the energy
of ocean-waves upon a still canvas.

I present my heart like a begging bowl.
He gives me a taste of eternal bliss.

In the Dark of the Moon

In the dark of the moon
I call to Sai, "Lead me from this labyrinth.
Deliver me from this cold cave of confusion."

"The Kali Yuga will soon end," he tells me.
  "Kali tries to teach you now.
    Remember Chaucer?
  Remember the Wife of Bath?"

"But I am a woman!" I protest.

"Embrace the Crone," he answers.
"She is you and so is Botticelli's Venus.
  Start your day with goddess love;
    end the day with goddess light."

Calcutta

Around the dusty walls
Of the dim hotel room,
I am alone with my sick friends' faces
And the world outside the window.
The sheds' posts are the only tree I see.
It rained last night
And the men are re-collecting discarded plastic
For women to sew new roofs.
Children stamp mud into place.
They were born on this street
And will probably die here.

Dave moans. I sponge him with alcohol.
Chris' lips are blue. I check his pulse for silence.
Last week, we discussed soul journeys
On a Himalayan foothill.
Last night he was delirious.
The light bulb contrasted the black outside.
Rain stuck to the window like seeds.
I have despaired of the doctor's arrival.
Here, pain is endured, not defeated.
A death gives space for three births.

Cremation

I ran down the hill with my camera,
Thinking how the picture would sell.
I studied the weight in my hand
And waited for the small crowd to reach
The river bank.
I focused the lens.

Four men supported a wrapped body
Covered with flowers.
A young woman stood stiffly below,
The children clinging to her sari.
The weeping people were old.

As a fire formed
A midday sunset upon the water,
And the smoke made a fog curtain,
I capped my lens.
The crowd changed
As if to cover up
The sound of cracking bones.

Unlike her ancestors, the woman
Stood away from the pyre.
Like Penelope, she knew he would return.

First Darshan

That morning I misplaced my mirror.
I took my water ration,
Bathing and rinsing from the same bucket.
One of my roommates put aside her book of Vedas
And impatiently folded and pinned my sari.

Feeling the crucifix between my breasts,
The same crucifix I felt
Stepping off the train in Belfast,
I took my place beside
a blonde in a meditation pose –
False eyelashes curling over her closed lids.
The other woman seemed fetal-eyed.
Across the room, the men were stiff
And military in their white outfits.

An Indian man with a woman's voice
Led the bajan-songs.
A woman with a pierced nose
Played the harmonium.
My throat tightened.

Suddenly, the orange robe of Sai Baba
Glided across the platform.
I strained my eyes to meet his.
Sweat pasted my sari to my skin.

"There is only one religion, the religion of love."
"There is only one caste, the caste of humility."
"There is only one ..."

"One … all … all is God ..."

My thoughts drifted home. It must be a cold night.
For a second I felt the warmth of coffee mugs
And the laughter of friends joining me for a study-break.
Their understanding faces helped me trace
The premises of my newly discovered possible truths.

Watching the kaleidoscopic tray
Of flowers and sweet prashad being passed,
I thought of Daniel refusing the Babylonian wine.
I took the Communion, holding the sticky candy
In my palm.

Surrounded but alone,
I returned to my sleeping bag and books.

To Baba

You spoke to me
but I misplaced your words.
You said, "Seek the God within."
I thought you were absurd.

I thought I could run from you
I thought I could escape.

I pursued false premises
I stalked false promises
My tongue felt thirst
a craving to be heard.

I did not know the thirst
was really your absence!

Like Arjuna's brothers I drank
from the cool lake of desire.
Like Narcissus, my false reflection captured me.
I echoed my own nonsense.

But in the dark of the moon
I called to you.
I took one step; you took 1,000.
You said, "Seek the God within."
I seek the God within.

The Return

Circa Christmas 1975

The last days, I avoided
The ashram's piss-smelling showers,
Then plunged into the walls
And lights of airports and airplanes.

At home, between cool sheets,
I'm still crossing the Atlantic
With a life preserver underneath.
I have arrived wrapped and somewhat yellow
Like a stale newspaper.
    Beside the door, a duffel bag
Holds saris and my journal.
In the closet, my clothes
Hang like costumes.
They belong to the diploma on the wall –
The award for spending nights
Probing B. F. Skinner's dreams
and Sylvia Plath's nightmares.

Turning off the light,
I count the stars
Outside the window.
After months with a sleeping bag,
My bed is a new invention.

Alone With Candles

The flames sway down
like willow branches –
one by one a tear is quickly fossilized.
I count the time
by the millimeters of stalagmites.
Form, once again, becomes formless.

Above
in the dark
the fan and the dance of life –
Nataraja and the breath of life.

Gaea's Monologue

I remember being formless
In a chaotic universe.
My two parent planets
Had destroyed themselves
In my creation.
In the time when the stars shifted,
I would alternate a season of glaciers
With a season of sand and steam.
By the time Helios began his rule,
I had become spherelike,
Yet I was always I,
A waif in the beginning,
But never a child.
Alone, I grew into myself.

Artemis was once the smallest
Of three sisters.
They shadowed her from the stars,
So she was also the swarthiest.
She was pockmarked by the asteroids
From which she shielded the others.
As it came to pass,
The two older sisters
Melted over me,
Forming canyons and more rocks.
Volcanoes erupted and comets swam around.

Artemis glowed in Helios' image,
Becoming a queen with no one to rule.
A shell of rock and dust,
She glared at me
While slowly but carefully
I bore the seeds and eggs
Of my children's beginning.

Guinevere In The Abbey

I am now at peace

In my small room

With no firewood.

Christ is my only king;

Saint Michael my only knight.

The window is my mirror;

I suppose my eyes are still green.

The oaks, pruned of mistletoe,

Grow amid the moon

And season changes.

Some nights, in foolish dreams,

I am the golden-haired girl again,

Full of wine and dance,

Setting ordeals and posing for tapestries.

The the bell sounds; the horn's echo drifts.

At morning Communion,

The clay cup is my Grail.

That which bloomed red

Will soon be covered with white.

Worms, feeding upon the Round Table,

Await the feast day of my flesh.

They are no more frightening to me

Than the birds that devour

The last crumbs of my bread.

Barren, with a fertile soul,

I await my ascent.

Up at 6 (To Write, Of Course)

Staring into the black moon
of the coffee,
I wake before my nose hits.
The clock now reads 6:15.

Across the room
on my typewriter,
a half-printed sheet
waits like a kneeling saint.
The characters are giving her indigestion;
they're threatening a strike
unless I finish them.
The jealous lover
in the box of printed sheets
says he's going to burn
the box of clean sheets.

The ivy leaves droop
like drunken heads.
Did I water them yesterday,
or did my persona?

My eyes keep hooking
the black and gold
on the top shelf of the bookcase.
That old book of numerology!
Should I check to see
if today's a good day for writing?
No. I'm going to be a serious writer.
Maybe I should just read Sappho today.
No.

I gulp the cold coffee.

Sitting down at the desk,
I flex my fingers like a musician.
Outside, the cacophony of Helios' messengers.

Today's Horoscope

Pisces:

    Find a friend and take the day off.
    Have the shopping spree you intended
    Or play golf.

Aries:

    Money will come through a surprising sources.
    Just remember: positive thinking I the force.

Taurus:

    Use your charm to sell what must be sold.
    If charm fails, try being bold.

Gemini:

    You soon will be experiencing
    Fewer problems with your mate.
    Bring home wine and flowers.
    The argument should wait.

Cancer:

    Today's not a good day to feel despair.
    Stick to your diet. Make others care.

Leo:

    Take a subordinate position in business dealings.
    Rule from the middle. Trust your feelings.

Virgo:

    Try not being critical with yourself today.
    Relax. Have a drink. Engage in horseplay.

Libra:

    Venus is shining on your success.
    If you haven't yet found it, buy a new dress.

Scorpio:

    You are the manipulator of the horoscope.
    If someone stands in your way,

Try a practical joke.

Sagittarius:

Concentrate on making money
And investing more. Your family can wait:
They're the inheritors!

Capricorn:

You'll soon receive a call
From a long-lost love. Put away practicality.
Trust the stars above.

Aquarius:

You were born in the sign of the brand-new age.
Others will learn by your tutorage.

A Divorcee

The dawn after the first sleep,
She gathers herself like clay.
Soon, she must rearrange
The room weighted down on one side.

The face in the bathroom mirror
Tingles like a sleeping foot.
Closing the cubicle door,
She washes the bar smoke from her hair.
The ocean-shell echoes.

Awakened by the newspaper's thud,
She decides to move to the kitchen.
Over coffee, she'll study the want-ads.

Quietly, through the curtain,
The red sun becomes white.

In Media Res

I am a doctor of philosophy:
I know everything.

But what is everything?

What do you mean, "What is everything?"
Everything is a pronoun.
One pronoun can represent many different
people, places and things.

*Have you met everyone, traveled everywhere,
and done everything?*

MORNING AFTER LAST FROST

Buds lay stiff and dry
on branches   a snapped branch swings
down   Tarot's Hanged Man

Risk

If a sign read "Keep out,"
I entered.
Unlike Alice,
I never looked for skull & bone signs on bottles,
but by God's grace, I survived.

I could blame the 1970s
on my malignant curiosity
but I won't.
I blame myself and thank God
I have more than 9 lives.

I boarded a train from Dublin to Belfast
just to see if Northern Ireland
was as dangerous as it was on the news.
With three friends
I explored a city
resembling a mouth missing teeth.
Flirting soldiers held submachine guns.

NEST RHYME

Dough rises like a belly,
Through the window
Embryos of potatoes, carrots
Sleep in the garden
The cat licks her eggs and milk
While I boil pears
Into jelly

NIGHT MAGIC

Scent of rain and clear
Clouds gliding like ghosts
The moon sprouts through
the dark sky
like a mushroom

Oklahoma Memories

(Rhea McKnight, a journalist,

returns to her home town.)

Papa was proud to sell his land in '58.
He bought a car dealership
And we moved to town.
Looking at the mall's packed parking lot,
I guess the town has moved here.

At the edge, the farmhouse stubbornly stands,
Somewhat dignified
Now that the cracked paint is gone.
A lady in Tulsa was thrilled
To buy the windmill.

To the music of wind and birds,
I drummed a dance on this earth
Thinking about my Cherokee ancestors.

Sometimes the field hands brought their kids.
We'd chase the rabbits
And make mud pies with corn and leaves.
They left for cities and never returned.
The tenants ran the new drive-in.

It seemed that everyone joined
To worship the new –

Parades celebrated dialing telephones;
Crowds awaited drawings at T.V. stores.

Now, all I really see are
Cotton acres in their graves
Under tract homes and imported trees.

Rapunzel Alone

Veiled, I walk the gardens at noontide;
At night, moonlight soothes my hair-roots.
Motherless, I never learned
About men or needlepoint.

Men! My clever knave told me
I was the fairest.
He blinded himself rescuing me,
And I cured him.
Now he's kingdoms away snaring other blondes.
I'm told about Cinderella and Snow White before me!

A lady-in-waiting says
I should learn to weave like Penelope.
She says my prince will return
When my hair grows long again.

As for now, I am unable to run or ride.
If I knew alchemy,
I could melt the chastity belt –
I have become the tower, circled in thorns.

Relocation

I have moved my face

From apartment to apartment

Where others have shown passion

On the furniture and doors.

Each relocation begins

With the same ritual of scrubbing

Strangers' staph from the sinks and floors.

The junk mail greets me:

"Meet new neighbors at free keg party…"

"Free patty-melts through Friday…"

"Free drinks for wet T-shirts…"

"Free…"

After the chipped dishes are unwrapped,

I retire like dust behind curtains.

In the semi-dark, I explore

My new, simulated sky.

The last time, my eyes were caught

By crucifixion hooks

Where undoubtedly hung neurotic plants

That probably never knew

If the occasional gushes of chlorine water

Would be their last supper.

Sarah

*Sarah Stone Hill 1852-1868 and Infant Boy
Wife and Son of Andrew James Hill*

Your death date makes you both young and old.
You're the same age as a great-great grandmother
And as my giggly students.
Somehow, I picture you as blue-eyed and freckled,
With brown hair in a braided bun.
Your waist was innocent of corsets
And small until your child invaded your body.
No one told you how babies arrived
In this world, until your wedding night.
Your beloved Andrew became a barnyard animal.
You cried for Mother.

The next morning, the sun
Reflected on the new quilt.
It was warm for February.
Andrew gave you an armload of flowers
And your first cup of coffee.
You savored the smells,
Then unpacked your small trunk –
Aprons made from knitted rags,
A Bible and a silver spoon.
Finding flour, you baked bread
While Andrew hunted rabbits.
Later, he taught you
To shoot rattlesnakes and wolves.

Together, you began weekdays of hard work
And a Sabbath day of prayer.

Sometimes rain brought more weeds
And wind carried away chickens.
You only prayed harder.

Your last summer was dusty and hot.
Andrew sometimes forced you to eat.
Secretly, you fed the birds and rabbits
And took care not to disturb their nests.
Wading at the creek,
You felt the schools of fish nibble at your toes.
One day, the preacher's wife
Caught you with bare, wet feet.

Quickly, you fastened your shoes
And served her tea cakes.
She told you, "Children are gifts
From the Lord." She read you Genesis 3:16.
You were told to later miss prayer meetings,
And you were given a book of children's prayers.

Andrew could afford only one colored boy,
So you helped with the cotton picking.
Your sunbonnets matched the Mother Hubbards.
At the end of the day, you soaked
Your face and hands in buttermilk.
Soon your heavy body became accustomed to pain.
You could not sleep without work.

The harvest was bounteous that year.
Andrew promised you a big house someday.
You walked together in the breeze,
Crushing the crisp autumn leaves,
Watching the movements of clouds and birds.
The first cold day came in November.

You sewed bibs and roasted nuts by the cedars.

When your time came, a granny woman was with you.
Through tears, you watched the candlelight.
Andrew held your head as you choked on whiskey,
And gave you leather to bite.

The Bus Stop Girl

Where the caged pawn shops

Face the multi-colored bars,

And a sidewalk if ripped

By the roots of stumps,

A girl in a striped dress sits

At a bus stop weaving rags and singing.

Her chorus consists of traffic-roar,

And screams of children throwing rocks

In damp tunnels. Her song is

Accompanied by radios from tenements,

Where women sleep off the night

Or grow fat on canned spaghetti and beer.

Once, a black woman in a white dress

Touched the girl's shoulder.

She ran, stumbling into the garbage.

For a while she moaned,

And empty bottles rattled on the pavement.

The next day, the girl sat

At the bus stop, singing and weaving.

The Other Woman

The other woman is a paper doll.
I pick her up off the bathroom floor
every morning.
I gently close her, cover her.
Sometimes her eyes stare back at me,
sometimes they tease.
Sometimes she is blond,
sometimes Oriental.
She changes like the moon
but she is the same collective soul –
Lit up by gels and pimps' flattery
she pays rent –
a split-second fantasy
that lasts a month.

The Roots

A part of me is like roots –

Unseen trunks with tiny hair-twigs,

Meditating in a fetal sleep.

Sometimes I feel their scales

Stretching out into the darkness.

Solitary philosophers:

They understand both the desert

And the forest of me,

Keeping my balance

When the ground suddenly shifts.

For the Woman Whose Story I Read
On Page 14c

In a city section

Where roaches die of old age,

A woman sits in a locked room

With an open coathanger.

She must be quick;

Her child cries in another room.

Questions Few Ask
Haiku

What is a poten-
tial human if it's
already alive?

Reptilian brain
but even reptiles feel fear
and respond to pain.

Abortion

I became an orphan
that cold day
as if I wielded a ritual knife
and severed the umbilical core to God.

I lay 30 bills on one table
and lay down on another.

Jesus didn't burst in
and overturn either table
because I had cut him out of my heart.

Satan Is a Loser

When he raps
and flaps his leathery wings,
I feel no fear –
no threat in fallen things.

Self

I journeyed inside
but found no god.
Even the inner child was gone.
She had grown up
and found better things to do!

WOMAN AS MOON

The man is drunk
when you shine,
He cannot see you in the morning;
Only the reflection of himself
that he calls 'the hag.'

The Ex

Did he erase me
like a flash drive
or do I slip through
the white-out
like a mirror's ghost?

A Limerick for Mother

My mother sucked passion from books,
A few were written by cooks.
She loved Mickey Spillane
and tales of Lady Jane,
but thought Stephen King was a kook.

On a Trip to Grass Valley
a haiku

I wrote a great poem,
but Deborah's goat ate it;
I hope he's sated.

Zen Concrete

Teaching forces me to gather the abstract
and draw graphs and flow-charts
showing its relation to the concrete.
But graphs and flow-charts are also abstract,
so I look at my students' puzzled faces,
erase, and begin again.

When my parents married my mother
taught philosophy and pondered Bergson's views
on individuality and the self.
My father poured concrete for Brown and Root
and contemplated how changing weather
could or would affect the mixture.
Even pouring concrete isn't exactly
a concrete endeavor.

As an undergraduate, I meditated on
B. F. Skinner's dreams and Sylvia Plath's nightmares
or was it the other way around?
I wonder how B. F. Skinner would have handled
the sixth-grade boy who hid under my desk and cried?
It was my first teaching job,
and all I knew was Sylvia Plath.
In graduate school I swam upstream
with Deconstruction, then realized
that the stream itself my not exist.

I write all this while sitting on the hot concrete.
It exists because I feel it and see it.
Or is the concrete part of the Maya?

A Solo of Tranquility
written at age 15

The flowers around had long since died,
Lifeless was the countryside.
Though barren, Winter sang to me
A solo of tranquility.